Beyond Inspiration

14 Transformational Prayers to Increase
Your Impact & Influence

Melissa J. Nixon

Damian Johnson / Nicole S. Mason / Lynette Dutton / Jade Simmons
Lana Hunter / Kelli K. Fisher / Kelly Janine Joyner / Youlisha Bundy
Cheryl Riley / Roshanda E. Pratt / Melissa Nixon / Otescia Johnson
Saundra Wall Williams / Charonda Johnson

Scripture taken from THE HOLY BIBLE, NEW INTERNATIONAL VERSION ®. Copyright© 1973, 1978, 1984, 2011 by Biblica, Inc.™. Used by permission of Zondervan

Scripture taken from the New King James Version®. Copyright © 1982 by Thomas Nelson. Used by permission. All rights reserved.

Scriptures taken from the HOLY BIBLE, NEW LIVING TRANSLATION, Copyright© 1996, 2004, 2007 by Tyndale House Foundation. Used by permission of Tyndale House Publishers, Inc., Carol Stream, Illinois 60188. All rights reserved. Used by permission.

Copyright 2019 by Melissa J. Nixon

All rights reserved. No part of this book may be reproduced or transmitted in any form or by any means, electronic or mechanical, including photocopying and recording, or by an information storage and retrieval, without permission in writing from author and publisher.

Printed in the United States of America
2019 First Edition

Subject Index:
Nixon, Melissa J.
Title: Beyond Inspiration – 14 Transformational Prayers to Increase Your Impact & Influence
    1. Inspirational 2. Purpose 3. Prayer 4. Christian

Paperback ISBN: ISBN: 978-1-7338051-5-5

courageouslifeacademy.com

Dedication

This book is dedicated to every leader and entrepreneur who dares to believe God for *more* in their life, career, or business. Your dreams are not too big.

"I am the LORD, the God of all mankind.
Is anything too hard for me?
Jeremiah 32:27

Table of Contents

Introduction 7

Dare to Believe You Are Embarking on a New Journey
Nothing Happens Until We Move — Damian Johnson — 14
Pace Yourself — Nicole S. Mason — 22
God is Doing a New Thing Now — Lynette Dutton — 32
It's a New Era — Jade Simmons — 43

Dare to Believe You Are Filled and Still Growing
Fill My Cup — Lana Hunter — 56
Going Beyond — Kelli K. Fisher — 64
Going from Good to Fertile Ground — Kelly Janine Joyner — 79

Dare to Believe You Are Winning, and Changing the Game
Leading While Bleeding — Youlisha Bundy — 89
The Game Changing Shot — Cheryl C. Riley — 102

Dare to Believe You Are Worthy, Approved, and Established
Dare to Believe God You are Worthy — Roshanda E. Pratt — 115
Dare to Believe You Are Approved — Melissa J. Nixon — 122
Established in Prayer — Otescia R. Johnson — 131

Dare to Believe You Are Prepared for the Next Level
How to Pray for Your Next Level — Saundra Wall Williams — 143
The Next Level of Greatness Through Service — Charonda Johnson — 158

Acknowledgements

Introduction

Have you ever felt so confident that God was calling you to make a bigger impact and have an even greater influence in the world? However, the distance between what you felt and what He showed you seemed like light years away? I have an inkling that if you are reading this book, you have. The truth is that we are *each* called to make a lasting impact while we are here - one that extends beyond human metrics, accolades, and awards. Having social media influence, followers, or a high number of video views is great for visibility but does not necessarily translate into transformational impact. The type of impact and influence that transforms systems and changes nations. It's the type of things I think about when it says in the word that we would do greater works than what Christ did while He was here (John 14:12). Yes, that scripture applies to *you* too, it applies to all of us. It's a stretching passage because while when many of us first read it we wondered what in the world could that be? And while that question of wonder has been around for years, I personally wonder if the answer lies in us fulfilling the very things on earth that God thought about as He was forming us in our mother's womb? I'm talking about the things we talk ourselves out of every day, don't move with the speed we need to, or live up to the of greatness we know that we have. The *greater things* may very well be things that extend beyond *your* human comprehension but lie well within the supernatural gifts, creativity, and ability He placed in you.

As a believer, leader, and entrepreneur, I firmly believe there is a life and impact we are supposed to live and experience well beyond the status quo and day to day of our existence. A level that even exceeds the successes everyone applauds you for and wishes they could achieve. It would be easy for you to stop right here because where you are is farther than most people even reach. You have been able to achieve more than most in your family, a good portion of your classmates, *and* you've exceeded a number of the goals you set yourself. And let's face it, you have even achieved some things you didn't have the audacity to believe for. But even with all of your success, stopping where you are today would feel like a failure because you signed up for impact not just comfort and accolades.

So, now it's time to fill the gap. The gap is the void or ache you feel between your successes of today and the earth-shaking influence you *know* you can really have tomorrow. Those feelings of discontentment exist because deep down inside you know you are part of the solution to something bigger...to the type of change the world really needs. Unlike others, your desire for more visibility, money, and connections isn't selfish but strategic. You understand that those things are tools that open doors and create seats at tables.

One of the reasons many leaders and entrepreneurs pause before racing to new and accelerated levels is because they understand that each new level comes with an even greater level of responsibility. We often feel the weight of what we're walking into before it happens. Even as you read this book, you can feel the responsibility not just for where you are now, but where you are going. That's because we know in order to have impact and influence we can't just sit idle but or just bet at the table but we need to lead it, change it, and transform it. As believers, we understand that even if there are laws, processes, people or systems in place that seem insurmountable to overcome, we serve a supernatural God who can do *all* things through *us* – the greater things.

Knowing the weight of that responsibility can feel daunting at times, my heart is always extended to other leaders and entrepreneurs on how to carry both the weight and the wait. You know, the period between when God downloads the vision and when you start fully walking in it. God often downloads to me ways to keep them/me/us encouraged, walking by faith, and moving us from our comfort zone to our zone of influence where true change happens and legacy grows even deeper. One particular download was to host a prayer call one year on New Year's Day. But not just a call where people would call in for thirty minutes or an hour… a 12-hour prayer call from 6am to 6pm!

When the idea first came to me, it took my breath away. I wondered how in the world it would come together. Looking back, it was fairly easy, but during the process it seemed almost insurmountable because it was unchartered territory, at least for me. Not only did everyone I ask to participate and lead a 30-minute prayer segment say yes, but people called in. What was a big vision in my mind was actually too small. I thought people would call in for 30 minutes here or there throughout the day. Little did I know, what was about to transpire would change the trajectory of not only people's year but their life. Listeners not only got on for 30 minutes but they could not get off. Some of them stayed on the line praying with us for four, six, or even eight hours. What was supposed to be a day of running errands for some turned into cancelled plans and perfectly tuned ears to what God was saying through each of the prayer leaders that day. It was a divine appointment.

The entire experience blew me, no, us away and the testimonials that came afterward definitely created many, "Wow, God!" moments for myself and others. As we were praying that day, I knew that the powerful devotionals being shared were not just for that moment or for that audience but were for you too – the leader; the entrepreneur who dares to believe that God can and will use them to create transformational shifts wherever He leads you to go. One of the listeners told me months later that it felt like she was in the middle of a revival because her life changed so much since that day of prayer and surrender. As you read this book, my prayer for you is not only a revival in your personal life but in each of your areas of influence. I pray that you not only experience a revival in your heart and relationship with God but that you experience transformation in the level of impact you have in the world.

Each of the prayer leaders who participated that day and are sharing their powerful devotions and prayers with you are accomplished leaders and entrepreneurs in their industries of business, education, personal development, ministry, real estate, and more. More importantly, they carry the heart of God, which is why I believe that day was not just a day a prayer but a move of God. It had nothing to do with my God-idea and everything to do with their yes and sharing God's heart with the world.

You may have picked up this book because you are longing to create even greater impact in the areas of influence God has given you. You may have picked it up because you are wondering how do you execute and implement the things that have been etched in your heart but seem bigger than you. Each of these insightful devotions are not only filled with personal stories of transformation from the authors' own careers and businesses but supplemented with related scriptures and practical questions to further your own transformation.

You will also find that the book is divided into 5 key sections to encourage and prepare your heart for the level of impact that God wants to do in and through you. As you read this book,

We dare to believe you are ...

- Embarking on a new journey
- Filled and still growing
- Winning and changing the game
- Worthy, approved, and established
- Prepared for the next level

In each of these sections you will find the thoughts, prayers, and fiery words of the authors to push you to an even deeper level of impact. At the end of this book, impact and influence will be inevitable because:

- How you show up will be different.
- How you think will be different.
- How you act will be different.
- How you pray will be different.

Beware, creating the kind of transformation that God has shown you in your prayers and dreams goes beyond wonder, excitement, and wishful thinking. It cost. It will take focus, sacrifice, discipline, perseverance, and faith. It will also take an even greater understanding that everyone will not understand your new or evolved way of thinking, praying, or working. But you are not here to win friends, you are here to win and impact the world. Ghandi, Mother Theresa, and many of the spiritual giants who have gone before us like Kathryn Kuhlman, George Muller, and William Seymour all had to go through the same thing. If you haven't heard their names, go ahead, look them up and read about the influence they had and the impact they made on history.

Your purpose is bigger than you. It's bigger than providing for your family. It is the place of existence that lies beyond knowing that you are called and truly walking in your calling. It extends beyond being excited about the vision God gave you to being willing to sacrifice and do the work. Leaders that get this, while they may pray for a roadmap, take action to the what they know God is telling them to do today. When God said pray, there was no book idea. What I thought would help someone for 30 min at the top of the year turned into hours, a personal revival for attendees, and now a book that will have global impact organizations and nations well beyond our years.

As you begin this journey of daring to believe God for more impact and more influence, don't be intimidated by the outcome. Instead, be adamant about the very next thing He has given you insight to do today.

Yes, you were created for such a time as this (Esther 4:14), now,

Dare to Believe God,

...and ACT!

Dare to Believe…

You Are Embarking on a New Journey

Nothing Happens Until We Move

Damian Johnson

On the day of prayer, as I sat listening to the words spoken and the prayers prayed by all the women who spoke before me, I felt God quickening my spirit because so much of it paralleled what He gave me to share. Despite being the only man on the prayer call, I was truly humbled to be a part of and blessed by the experience.

Movement. That's the idea God wanted me to share. Maybe you've gone through a lot in the last year and maybe you have great expectations for what the next year will be, what you will do, and what you are believing God for. But nothing happens until we first MOVE.

When you look at scripture and study all of the great patriarchs and people of faith found in the Word, everything they accomplished had to do with them taking action **FIRST**. The story of the four lepers illustrates this perfectly.

2 Kings 7:3-9 NASB

> Now there were four leprous men at the entrance of the gate; and they said to one another, "'Why do we sit here until we die?" "If we say, 'We will enter the city,' then the famine is in the city and we will die there; and if we sit here, we die also. Now therefore come, and let us go over to the camp of the Arameans. If they spare us, we will live; and if they kill us, we will but die." They arose at twilight to go to the camp of the Arameans; when they came to the outskirts of the camp of the Arameans, behold, there was no one there. For the Lord had caused the army of the Arameans to hear a sound of chariots and a sound of horses, *even*

the sound of a great army so that they said to one another, "Behold, the king of Israel has hired against us the kings of the Hittites and the kings of the Egyptians, to come upon us." Therefore, they arose and fled in the twilight, and left their tents and their horses and their donkeys, *even* the camp just as it was, and fled for their life. When these lepers came to the outskirts of the camp, they entered one tent and ate and drank, and carried from there silver and gold and clothes, and went and hid *them*; and they returned and entered another tent and carried from there *also*, and went and hid *them*. Then they said to one another, "We are not doing right. This is a day of good news, but we are keeping silent; if we wait until morning light, punishment will overtake us. Now therefore come, let us go and tell the king's household.

In the background of this story, there is a horrendous famine all over the land. The famine was so horrific, that in the chapter before the story of the four lepers, women were boiling and eating their children, some people were paying money for a donkey's head to use as food, and others were eating dove's dung. It was a torturous time and there were no resources anywhere in the land. In addition to all that was happening in society at the time, the lepers had been labeled as outcasts and were required to sit outside of the city gates and separate themselves from the people who lived inside the city. As they sat stuck outside the city gates observing the famine and accepting the reality that everyone was about to die, they asked themselves, "Why are we still sitting here?" This question leads them to get creative and take a risk. In their situation, they did not fear going to the enemy's camp, because *what's the worst that could happen?*

As you consider the many roles and responsibilities you have in your life and in your business, **where are you sitting stuck, like the lepers, with the vision God has given to you?** When you figure out where you are just sitting, next let me ask, **why are you still sitting there?**

Some of you, like me, are stuck because we suffer from Imposter Syndrome, which is the belief that we aren't good enough because we haven't yet produced the result that proves we are good enough. We've been labeled by mistakes from our past and haven't yet arrived at the place we believe we should be. Even though the Imposter Syndrome isn't real, the mental tape we play in our minds about ourselves has detrimental effects on our productivity and purpose. It may be hard to acknowledge, but I'm confident that God has given each of us a vision and a plan. Now, all we need to do is *execute*.

2 Timothy 1:7 NASB

> For God has not given us a spirit of timidity [fear], but of power and love and discipline.

Somewhere, deep down, there may also be a creeping fear that says, *"If I step out, more is going to be required of me, so I'll just stay put."* If you're thinking that, you are absolutely right. Living and operating at the next level of faith in your life and business will require more discipline and more responsibility. God is waiting on you to overcome the fear of living with greater accountability and higher expectations – no one is ever ready for it, but everyone who yields, is always better because of it.

Where is fear causing you to procrastinate and rely on excuses? Where is fear preventing you from taking action that you know you *could* take to move yourself forward?

We will never get the results that God wants for us, and more importantly, God will never get the glory until we move past our fear and step into what He is calling us to do by faith.

The lepers took a risk when they moved. At that time, they had no knowledge of how the Lord was also moving on their behalf. The Lord had already gone before them and moved their enemy out of the way. When the lepers arrived at the camp, the enemy was already gone. Could it be that the Lord is waiting for you to move FIRST before you see the result of His activity in your life and business? Whether you are in the early phase of entrepreneurship or you already have an established business, there is more action you need to take to move into the next level.

What I love most about the story of the lepers is, even though the lepers were the first ones to discover the abandoned camp of the enemy, after they had gotten their bellies full, ate, drank, and taken all the silver, gold, and clothes they wanted (including a hidden stash), the lepers decided to tell the king about their discovery so that others could benefit from the spoil the enemy left behind. You taking your business to the next level, you writing that book, you starting that blog, you creating that product – it really isn't about you. There are people whose lives are dependent on you stepping into your purpose. Your assignment is bigger than you. There is something that God is trying to fulfill in, with, and through you for the benefit of other people. Who might never be blessed if I never take that next step forward? Who might remain stuck because I'm too afraid to move into what God has for me? When God gives you a blessing, it's never just about you. Yes, He wants us all to be blessed, but we are blessed to be a blessing.

Each morning, when the sun comes up and my feet hit the ground, I've got to move. Otherwise, somebody is not going to receive the blessing that they should have because I refused to show up. If you think about that, it's a haunting thought.

James 1:22-25

> But prove yourselves doers of the word, and not merely hearers who delude themselves. For if anyone is a hearer of the word and not a doer, he is like a man who looks at his natural face in a mirror; for *once* he has looked at himself and gone away, he has immediately forgotten what kind of person he was. But one who looks intently at the perfect law, the *law* of liberty, and abides by it, not having become a forgetful hearer but an effectual doer, this man will be blessed in what he does.

The Lord has given you an anointing. There is something that you find easy to do that is difficult for other people. As you step past your fear and bring forward what the Lord is calling you to do – what He's put in your hands to do – then not only will you be blessed, but other people will be blessed because of you. The work you are called to do matters. Take your eyes off of yourself long enough to believe God and give Him the benefit of the doubt. What if God really blows your mind? Sometimes, when we think about launching a business or taking our business to the next level, we think about all the things that could go wrong. But do we ever spend any time thinking about what could go right? What if God breathes on your efforts? What if He really does exceedingly, abundantly above all you could ask or think? What if God moves on your behalf? It is time to MOVE. It's time out for thinking and being in fear. It's time out for procrastinating and being undisciplined. It's time to bring forward what God has placed in your heart.

If you're really honest with yourself, you know at least one thing you could do. If you did that one thing, it would move your business forward. Get into action mode. There are people and lives depending on you and waiting for you to bring forward the gifts God has given you. My prayer is that the Lord blesses you as you walk in obedience and move forward with what He's called you to do.

Prayer:

Father, I come in the name of Jesus, and first ask for forgiveness. All of us have done things that we shouldn't have done and said things that we shouldn't have said. Forgive us for our disobedience, forgive us for not acting upon the ideas and the visions you have given to us. Forgive us for stopping short. Please wipe the slate clean for us all, Father – we seek your forgiveness because we want nothing to hinder our prayers and your activity in our lives.

Holy Spirit of the Living God, we ask that you be present with us right now and speak to our hearts and minds. You have placed a seed of greatness inside of us and we want to nurture that seed so we can bear fruit. We sense your desire to birth something in and through us this year. Please help us overcome the voices of our doubts, our limiting beliefs, and our self-judgment. Cancel every voice that comes from lack and scarcity thinking and especially those that suggest that "I am not good enough" and cause me to question my worthiness. Lord, strengthen my hands and give me hands and feet that are swift to move.

I'm praying that we would begin to see you and your purpose in our lives as being the main thing. Let your purpose become so big that we cannot escape it and so that we will begin to move toward it. Push us, grow us, stretch us, take away the distractions and competing commitments, and make it so that we have no choice but to move into what you've called us to do. We know that is it not by might, nor by power, but by your Spirit. We are asking for you to fill us with a greater portion of your Spirit and activate us to bring forward the vision and the dream into physical manifestation. We believe we have the power within us to become who you've called us to be and do, what you have assigned us to do, and be the blessing in the earth. We believe you have called us to be the answer to someone's prayer.

I pray for every person holding this book and reading this prayer. You know us by name and you are the author and perfecter of our faith. You know every excuse, every alibi, every fear, and every doubt that we have used and allowed to restrict our movement. We ask for wisdom and guidance and ears to hear you. We will be still and listen for your still small voice as you whisper strategies and ideas. We are believing you for the directions and connections we need, so that as we take each step by faith, we will do so with the confidence that you are specifically and intentionally guiding us. We know that prayer is good, and praising you is even greater, but now we have to move. Order our steps Lord. Even when we aren't sure, I pray you help us learn to give you the benefit of the doubt. We know that you love us Lord. We know that eyes have not seen, ears have not heard, and nor has it entered into the heart of man all the good things that you have in store for us and all that you want to do through us.

You can do exceedingly abundantly above all that we can ask or think or even imagine. That's what we want for our lives and our businesses. I pray that we and our lack of movement are not the reasons that prohibit you from taking us to the next level. Help us to begin to think about the action we are going to take and how we're going to glorify you. Help us to walk in obedience, and in the process, activate our faith and take the necessary action steps to build our business and dominate the marketplace.

Lord, it's time to move and we pray that you keep this at the forefront of our minds and allow us to move and become everything you've called us to become. We love you. We thank you. We bless you. We honor you. We ask that you hear this prayer, in Jesus name, Amen.

Questions for Reflection:
- Proverbs 3:5-6 commands us to trust in the Lord and not our own understanding and that as we acknowledge him in all our ways, he will direct our paths. Have you given your ideas / plans to God through prayer?
- What is one thing you can do right now to move one step closer to your goal? By when will you do it?
- Accountability is the glue that ties commitment to results. Have you invited someone into your journey to remind you of what you said you would do and why?
- When something is important to you, it shows up in two places, your datebook and checkbook. What does your calendar and bank statement reveal about your level of intentionality?

Bio

Damian Johnson joined the John Maxwell Team in 2011. He is an Executive Director with the JMT and serves on the President's Advisory Council and is the Founder & CEO of Mandeville Ingleside LLC.

With dynamic interpersonal and sales skills as a Program Coordinator for the John Maxwell Team, Damian is bright, passionate and successful about enrolling new members into the JMT experience. In his latest role as a Peer Teaching Partner (PTP), Damian is your guide into all facets of the JMT experience and will invest valuable time adding invaluable insight, encouragement and vigilantly follow up with you.

As an International Speaker and Trainer, Damian has trained leaders internationally in Costa Rica and Liberia. He graduated from Morehouse College with a career in the banking, finance and mortgage industries.

Damian lives in Charlotte, NC with his wife Kendra and their two daughters.

Pace Yourself

Elder Nicole S. Mason, Esquire

Congratulations! I am so excited for you! This was a long time coming! These are the salutations we receive when we start a new job, embark upon a new journey, project, or initiative. It is in fact the newness that makes us feel good, and we have so much enthusiasm. We are upbeat, have a positive attitude, and we feel like we can conquer the world. But shortly thereafter, the motivation wanes, our attitude is slightly off or negative, and our energy is low. We really see this, or perhaps have even experienced it ourselves, when we enter in a new year. We make our resolutions. We are excited. We are pumped up and ready to go. However, by March, or sometimes, no… a lot of times, the momentum and motivation is gone before the end of January! Grab a cup of tea and let me tell you what happened to me in 2018, when I started something new at the beginning of the year.

I was asked to join a running group that would be training for a 5k. All the members in the group were running competitively for the first time. The name of the program was, "From Couch Potato to 5K." That should give you some indication that all the members were starting from the bottom. I laugh, even as I type this experience to share with you, to think of my actions on the very first day of training. The first thing you should know is the training began in January, which is the dead of winter in the DC Metropolitan area. So, I dressed for the low temperatures. In addition to the cold air, the park that we were training in was pitch black at 6:00 am. Ok, our passion and zeal can lead us into uncharted territory and sometimes leave you asking yourself, "What have I gotten myself into now?" That is a conversation for another time! I want to stay on task to encourage you with the three things you need to do to pace yourself and achieve your purpose

Control Your Breathing

So, we meet for the very first day of training, and I decide to take off down the trail like I am running a sprint. Wrong move! Then, I find myself starting to overheat. What is going on here? Then, shortly after I began running, of course, I was out of breath. Really Nicole!? To go a longer distance requires slow, consistent, and steady steps. Learning to control your breathing is paramount. You see, my running coach taught me how to slow myself down, get a steady rhythm, and to slowly build my endurance and momentum. So, it is with us in our lives, when we are excited about getting started and moving on various projects that we are working on. We must learn to slow down, get a rhythm, and control our breathing.

In 2 Chronicles 20, we meet King Jehoshaphat who finds himself facing an attack of monumental proportions from several neighboring enemies. His first response is panic. For most people, our first response to anything out of sorts in our lives is panic. King Jehoshaphat's next move is instructive for us. He calls the people that he is leading and tells them to fast and to pray. In other words, let's slow down, assess the situation, and respond differently.

It is hard to focus and get a grip on situations in our lives when we are moving too fast. I began to understand that controlling my breathing while running was vitally important, if I wanted to enjoy the training program and finish what I started. If I continued or tried to continue through the following weeks the same way I started, I would have likely quit. So many times, we don't allow ourselves to slow down and assess the situations in our lives, recalibrate ourselves, and then keep going. It is much easier to just stop and focus on the next project or initiative. This is the time for you to decide to see the projects you are working on all the way to the finish line. Tell yourself that there will not be any more starts and stops. Fulfilling purpose requires slow, steady, and consistent movement.

Constant Cadence

Once you control your breathing, it is important to maintain a constant cadence. I learned this word during my training. Cadence is simply movement. Cadence involves rhythmic movement. I learned first and foremost that a runner must have the proper shoes. So, it is important that we have the proper tools, resources, and people to focus on our assignments. Since none of us are experts in all things, it is important to bring the right people in to complement the areas where you may be weak or deficient. I know it may be hard to fathom that you have some weaknesses and deficiencies, but the reality is, we all have them. So, get over yourself and stay focused on the finish line.

Cadence helps the runner avoid injuries. In an effort to help me run at the right pace, my running coach told me about this application (app) that would help me set my tone and maintain my rhythm. God, in turn, also helps us by providing everything we need right at our fingertips. It is amazing to understand that there is a solution to every issue or problem that may arise in our lives, even before we need it. The Bible is full of solutions. There isn't a problem that will arise that the Bible doesn't have an answer for. Studying the Word of God requires cadence – a consistent rhythm that keeps us moving in spite of obstacles and assures us of the ability to maintain our momentum.

The thing that I love about cadence is that each person has a different rhythm. It is important to find the rhythm that works for you and do not ever compare yourself to others. Your cadence must be in alignment with who you are, what God has called you to do, and what God has given your hands to do in the Earth.

Consistent Movement

As you implement and execute purpose in your life, let this be the time you have consistent movement. You must understand that there is a huge difference between retreating at pivotal points and stopping. When one retreats, they are attempting to catch their breath, gain strength, and get back in the ring of life. The mindset is intentional on keeping it moving. On the other hand, when someone stops, that's just it, they stop! Consistent movement is just that, consistent – even movement at a slower pace – is movement. Ecclesiastes 9:11 says, "The race is not given to the swift …"

It is in our consistent movement that we come to learn about ourselves. During my training, I learned that dressing for the cold did not help me as I moved along the running trail. In fact, contrary to my own belief, all of the layers of clothing worked against me and not for me. What I didn't know was that my body heats up quickly. So, I had to remove layers but continue to move.

This reminds me of the encounter David had when Saul recommended that David wear Saul's armor going to battle against Goliath in 1 Samuel 17.

> *"Then Saul clothed David with his armor; he put a bronze helmet on his head and clothed him with a coat of mail. And David girded his sword over his armor. Then he tried to go, but could not, for he was not used to it. And David said to Saul, I cannot go with these, for I am not used to them. And David took them off."* (1 Samuel 17:38-39 AMP)

It is important to know what will help you to operate at your maximum capacity, as you move forward in what you have been called to do. Yes, you will be uncomfortable at times. At other times, you will feel like throwing in the towel. Still yet at other times, you will ask yourself, "Is it really worth it!?" In those moments, your **Why** has to be bigger than your discomfort. As I was preparing to run my first 5k, my "why" was about using the pain of losing my Mom to heart disease and being diagnosed myself a short time after my mother's death, to serve as an example to other women that you can take control of your health and win.

My "why" was to continue to focus on my own health by building endurance and affirming to myself that I could take on the challenge of running and win. It is important to note here that I ran my first 5k on June 9, 2018, and controlled my breathing, ran with a constant cadence, and had consistent movement, at times slowly, but I finished the race in 44 minutes!

David, too, was successful when he decided to stick to what he knew about himself. He decided that he wasn't going to use Saul's armor to go to battle.

> *"Then David took his staff in his hand and chose five smooth stones out of the brook and put them in his shepherd's [lunch] bag [a whole kid's skin slung from his shoulder], in his pouch, and his sling was in his hand, and he drew near the Philistine. When the Philistine came forward to meet David, David ran quickly toward the battle line to meet the Philistine. David put his hand into his bag and took out a stone and slung it, and it struck the Philistine, sinking into his forehead, and he fell on his face to the earth. So, David prevailed over the Philistine with a sling and with a stone, and struck down the Philistine and slew him."* (1 Samuel 17:40; 48-50b AMP)

Yes, I know that things get tough for us all. However, God is depending on us to be consistent and show up great, even when we are faced with what seems in the moment like insurmountable odds that are stacked against us. I know what that feels like to have your heart blown into a million pieces, but still have to control your breathing, have a constant cadence, and consistent movement. I went to sleep one night with a mom, only to wake up the next day and she was gone. My mom passed away in her sleep of a heart attack. Suddenly and unexpectedly, my whole life changed in an instant. I know what it feels like to have to retreat to catch your breath. I also know what it looks like when your "Why" has to take the lead in your life to keep you on track and on purpose.

Beyond Inspiration

My "Why" was looking me dead in the eye and posing the question, "What are you going to do now? Are you going to stop, or are you going to get back up, move forward and pace yourself through the pain?" I decided that I was going to do just that – get back up, find my cadence, and keep moving. God has used and continues to use every ounce of my pain related to losing my mom to be a blessing to so many others. Now, in that time it certainly didn't feel good and at times it still doesn't. I knew that the mandate on my life was much bigger than the pain I was experiencing. And sure enough, here I am just past the 13-year marker, and I've never stopped preaching or teaching. I have learned to pace myself, know when to retreat to catch my breath, but continue to move.

This reminds me of the day of my 5k, there is a sweet victory that comes along with staying the course and staying with God through difficult and dark times. On the day of the race, there were people everywhere. The Lawyers Have Heart Race is one of the largest competitive races each year in Washington, DC. As I stood there, pumped up and ready to start the race, the more advanced runners were in the front of the line. And trust me, there were lots and lots of advanced runners. Then, there were those that were behind them, including me. A great thing happened to me, as I set out on this new endeavor of running my first 5k. People were all around me, some of the people passed me. Some other people started walking shortly after the race started. The advanced runners were heading back to the finish line, almost immediately after the race started, it seemed. But then, I heard God whisper in my heart, "Nicole, run your race. Don't look to the left or the right, run your race." I had my music on with the tempo in my ear to keep my cadence strong and steady. I kept repeating what God said to me, "Nicole, run your race. Nicole, run your race. Nicole, run your race." I want you to include your name and say that to yourself, as I pray for you.

Nicole S. Mason

My Prayer for You

Father, in the name of Jesus, we thank You for this awesome opportunity to come boldly before Your throne of grace. Thank You for the Word that You have given us, as we embark upon new endeavors and new opportunities to pace ourselves. We thank You for loving us enough to give us a word for what lies ahead of us. What a mighty God You are. You are awesome, and we love You with everything in us. We don't take You or our relationship with You for granted. Thank You for being our God. Thank You for sitting high and looking low and knowing what we need, even before we need it. We honor You, and we are most grateful for Your love and Your loving kindness towards us.

Father, we pray for Your guidance and direction. Please move in our lives in the way that You see fit to move. Help us to stay the course with steady and consistent movement. We don't want to move out of turn but when You tell us to move. Give us the courage to move at Your voice and not allow our flesh to get the best of us in those moments. Help us to pull on our faith files and our holy highlights of what You've already done for us in the past and use those moments to push us forward. Help us to see that surely if You've done it before, You can do whatever we need You to do today. Give us the strength to appropriately apply our faith to each and every situation in the mighty name of Jesus.

Father, we pray for focus as we move forward. Give us what we need to pace ourselves for every project that You assign to us. Help us not to get distracted by others and what they're doing. Help us not to focus on the wins of others on social media and lose sight of our own wins and what You are calling us to do. We say a resounding YES to Your will and Your way for our lives. Thank You for every money-making idea and the witty inventions that You shall give us, as we move forward, and give us the courage to move forward on those things and provide the resources that we will need to bring them to pass.

We acknowledge that we are nothing without You and that we need You to help us do the impossible. We are most grateful for You moving us strategically in high places and causing us to speak truth to power. *Your Word says in Proverbs 1, "… Honest people are relaxed and confident, bold as lions."* (Proverbs 28:1, The Message Bible) Thank You that resilience and courage are in our DNA. We stand on the shoulders of mighty ancestors who have paved the way for us to have the kind of relationship that we have with You. They faced atrocities that we can only imagine in our minds, but yet they called on Your name and held onto their faith, giving us a blueprint of success for our lives today. Help us to never forget the rich history and legacy upon which we stand and those that lost their lives, so that we can have freedom to openly and publicly worship You.

We honor You for creating us in Your image and Your likeness. We are most grateful that You breathed Your very essence into us. We understand that Your Word says in Psalm 8,

> *"What is man that You are mindful of him, and the son of [earthborn] man that You care for him? Yet You have made him but a little lower than God [or heavenly beings], and You have crowned him with glory and honor. You made him to have dominion over the works of Your hands; You have put all things under his feet …"* (Psalm 8:4-6 AMP)

We are indeed assured that You have plans for us. We know that Your plans are not to harm us but to give us hope and an expected end. Jeremiah 29 says,

> *"For I know the thoughts and plans that I have for you, says the Lord, thoughts and plans for welfare and peace and not for evil, to give you hope in your final outcome. Then you will call upon Me, and you will come and pray to Me, and I will hear and heed you. Then you will seek Me, inquire for, and require Me [as a vital necessity] and find Me when you search for Me with all your heart."* (Jeremiah 29:11-13 AMP)

Father, thank You for the opportunity to pray and call on Your name. The righteous run therein and are safe. We are grateful to be able to communicate with You. Strengthen our prayer lives. Help us to make prayer a top priority in our lives. Thank You for consistently showing us that You not only hear us, but You respond to the prayers of our hearts. Help us all to make our time with You a habit, so that You might give us guidance and direction about our everyday living. Thank You for giving us strategy about our lives each day, so that we are victorious. Help us to know that even when we lose, we still win. We win, because we learn valuable lessons. We win, because we can use those lessons to help others that we meet along the way in our lives. Most importantly Father, help us all to pace ourselves to do what You have called us to do. Help us do it with excellence. Help us do with passion and zeal. Help us to do it with our Why forever in the forefront of our minds. All in all, help us to have consistent movement knowing that our testimony is the key to someone else's deliverance. We pray in the name of Jesus. Amen and Amen ... IT IS SO!

Questions for Reflection:
- What is your relationship with God?
- In what areas of your life do you need to pace yourself?
- What will you do to pace yourself?
- Why is pacing yourself important to you?

Bio
Nicole is a gifted writer, passionate attorney, powerful international speaker, and international best-selling author. Nicole earned Bachelor of Arts and Master of Divinity Degrees from Howard University. She also earned a Juris Doctor from the University of the District of Columbia David A. Clarke School of Law, a Master of Law from the George Washington University School of Law, and is a member of the Maryland State Bar.

She is a certified trainer, speaker and coach with the John Maxwell Team and an Executive Leadership Coach with an Executive Certificate in

Leadership Coaching from Georgetown University. Using her coaching skills, Nicole works with senior managers to enhance their workplaces and work diligently to increase diversity.

Nicole is a member the National Speakers Association, Women's Speakers Association, National Association of Professional Women, Federally Employed Women and the Georgetown University Network of Coaches. In addition, she has received numerous awards for her mentoring and development of women.

In her spare time, Nicole loves to read and write inspirational material. She is a contributing writer for various magazines and blogs. Her writing has been featured in over 300 media outlets around the world.

God is Doing a New Thing, Now

Lynette Dutton

I want to take our devotion from *Isaiah 43 18-19, "Forget the former things; do not dwell on the past. See, I am doing a new thing! Now it springs up. Do you not perceive it?"* You must know that God is doing a new thing in your life.

There are four areas God addresses in this scripture that I believe is the pattern you should use when He begins doing a *new* thing in you. First, *forget the former things* or the old ways, previous patterns. Past paradigms, limiting belief systems must be forgotten. We must renew our mind. In Romans 12:2 it talks about being transformed by the RENEWing of your mind. Let's renew our mind, so our belief systems don't limit us, allowing our mind to be enlarged to new possibilities, new ways of doing things, new strategies and structures to support all that God has for us.

Secondly, *don't dwell on the past,* this speaks more to the soul issues of our yesterday. Hurt, wounded emotions, & offense; we must be healed of these things that have been causing us to look behind at the pain instead of focusing forward at the possibilities. We can't dwell on the past, but we've got to dwell in His presence. We've got to dwell on what Christ is doing inside of us today. In Luke 5:37-38, "And no one pours new wine into old wineskins. Otherwise, the new wine will burst the skins; the wine will run out and the wineskins will be ruined. No, new wine must be poured into new wineskins." We need to think of our minds and hearts like the wineskins, we can't keep filling up on the *new* God wants to do in us with holes in our life from past hurt and offense. It'll cause leaks sabotaging our own success. We need to be whole!

Once we renew our mind and get our soul healed, we are in the position now to *See, God is doing a NEW thing.* Being whole gives us fresh vision where we can begin seeing that He's doing a new thing and He's doing it in and through us. This is where our thoughts and language become new to frame out the new creative thing God is doing. In the natural world we see then we say what we see, but in the Kingdom we speak then we see. Our words create our tomorrow, or what we will see.

Lastly in this verse it says, *do you not perceive it*. God is asking us if we can see how He sees. Do we have God's perception, are we seeing things from a heavenly or kingdom point of view. Once we forget old systems of thought, get healed from our past, get fresh Godly vision and speech, then we can perceive or become aware of dreaming and creating with God. In this time and season of newness we must also pray that our prophetic and discerning gifts be sharpened giving us a supernatural advantage in all we say and do.

Many of us have come from a place of limitations but we are about to enter an abundant place of overflow. God always brings us from the place of not enough, to the place of just enough, then finally to the promise land of more than enough. So today, I want you to decree that this is your year of supernatural manifestation.

- God is doing a New thing so we must Renew our mind
- Let go of the Past mistakes and limitations truly get our Soul healed
- Get fresh vision and clarity
- Think and Dream bigger God wants you taking territory

Prophetic Declarations

Here are some prophetic declarations you can say over your life, career, or business.

I decree and declare that Holy Spirit is driving you in life, leadership, and business. You're not being driven by the mandates of man, not driven by circumstances and situation, but right now Holy Spirit is breathing inside of you. The Great I Am is living inside of you. There is a fresh unction to go out and pursue all that He has given you. There's a faith and confidence coming upon you, like what came upon David when he faced that giant. Every enemy you will look at, and to every obstacle in front of you, you will say, give me this day, my daily giant because they are bread for me. They are strength for me. They are my public validation. I have had private validations and hidden victories long enough, now God is calling for us to shine and win. The mind of Christ come upon you for this new season of your life, for this New Year of your life.

Let your mind be renewed so you can be like the eagles and soar with higher heights in the year ahead. I know some of the blows that you took that made you weary and they made you feel like giving up or telling God, "I can't do it anymore." Today, there's a fresh strength rising inside of you. It is renewing you right now, renewing your strength as the eagle. Those things that have come, and crusted over your thinking, and crusted over your mind where you couldn't rise above the situation have now been broken off as we cross over into a new season. All of that stuff that has been clouding your judgment, that has been zapping your strength, that has been taking the energy of Christ out of you has been broken off of you, and behold, you have a new strength this day.

I decree and declare that new dreams are coming upon you, new ideas, and new strategies. There's even a new zeal upon you. I'm praying that a fresh baptism in the Holy Ghost come upon you this day and that there's a renewing of the nine gifts of the spirit in your life. This morning I release the fresh gifting of wisdom to be manifested in your life, the gift of knowledge, and the discerning of spirits! Oh, a new tongue be released in us today, for speaking in tongues and the interpretation of tongues be released in your life, that you will come into the working of all nine gifts of the spirit in your life, ministry, and business. The working of miracles, the gifts of healings, supernatural faith, and prophecy. I release a fresh wind of the spirit and a fresh immersion of the baptism of the Holy Spirit in your life today.

That you will not go two days, two weeks, two months, or into the next 10 to 12 months living in the old thing, but behold I speak a new thing, a fresh baptism, fresh giftings, a fresh unction, fresh dreams, fresh vision. I just heard God speak to you.

There's somebody that is reading this and God said, you're not dreaming big enough. You're dreaming what you can do, what man can do, but you have not added the supernatural components of Holy Spirit and of my presence to your dreams, and I am commanding you this day to dream bigger, to ask for more, and to think larger. God wants you to think and to operate supernaturally. He said one book is not enough. Two books are not enough. Five books are not enough. You need to start writing. One company is not enough. Two companies are not enough. Two locations are not enough. You need to start expanding. God is digging up some of your tent posts and pegs where you have been satisfied. You are right on the verge of your breakthrough and you've been satisfied. You feel like…

> *Yes! I'm finally going to be clear coasting now. God is finally doing this thing where I'm not going to have to worry so much. I'm not going to have to be concerned. I may not have to walk by faith so much because I'm going to be in the clear!*

That was my prayer yesterday morning. I just want to know. I want to be able to budget, I want to be able to plan, but God has bigger plans, so think bigger. Right now, He is taking a spiritual shovel to your tent pegs that you have dug deep in the ground and even cemented into your territory, and He is pulling them up and expanding you this very moment.

New dreams, new visions, new ideas, new strategies

I'm speaking supernatural strategies over you right now in Jesus' name, because there is no way you can do it on your own. It's going to take a sovereign Almighty God, the great I Am, to come into your dreams, plans, and strategies to accomplish what He has called you to do in Jesus' name. I thank you God. I decree and declare health and strength upon you this day. Health! Some of you have said, I would've been able to do so much more last year, but I didn't have the health. I didn't have the strength. I didn't have the fitness. I didn't have these things in my life operating. My joints hurt. I suffered from migraines. I suffered from arthritis. I suffered from debilitating illnesses. I suffered from my voice going out. I suffered from colds, sinuses, and allergies. I'm speaking supernatural healing through the airwaves to you today. Every evil disease and every symptom must bow to the name of Jesus.

Every situation must bow to the Almighty name of Jesus. Every doctor's report must bow to the name of Jesus. There is no name higher. The name of your doctor is not as great as the name of the great physician. The name of those people that have diagnosed you is not as great as the one who has healed you. Because in his word it says you were healed by his stripes. You were healed and I'm going to tell you when you are saved, when you are sanctified, when you are filled with the Holy Ghost, when you have the power of the blood of Jesus covering your life, no sickness or disease can take your life. So, I release the blessing of life and life more abundantly. I release no limitation on your strength and on your health in Jesus' name. Your allergies will bow, your sinuses will come into alignment with the Word of God! Cancer must bow to the name of Jesus. Diabetes must bow to the name of Jesus. Heart disease, high blood pressure, and high cholesterol must bow to the name of Jesus.

Tumors, lumps, and scars must dissolve in the presence of an Almighty God. Can I get an amen? I know I can't hear you right now, but I want you to say it wherever you are. I want you to say they must bow and I receive it. In this new season, supernatural healing, supernatural power is coming in your home, in your business, in your family, and those things will not be carried one step forward. Those things are being solved in the spirit realm this morning. This is a year of supernatural manifestation and angelic visitation. You may think that you're in your business just to make a dollar. You may just think you're in ministry because you can teach well or because you can sing well, but I'm going to tell you that there's an angelic visitation coming. Supernatural divine visitation is coming from God, and from those that he dispatches into your life, and it's going to cause supernatural manifestation that will erupt on all sides just like it did when Paul and Silas started praying in that prison cell. God's going to give you a call or he's going to give you a Paul or a Silas that can come and start praying and singing praises with you, whether it's in business, your home, ministry, or whether it's just a friend. You're going to be able to sing, and those prison bars are going to be loosed. Those bars are going to come down. Those prison doors are going to swing open. I'm going to tell you that the past that has been holding you captive and seems to hold you back, is breaking off of you supernaturally right now and you are set free in Jesus' name. I release divine strategies from Heaven. I release your ear to be able to hear the Holy Spirit. Even the still small uttering of Holy Spirit and the gentle nudging of Holy Spirit that you will become so acute, and so in tune to the moving of the Spirit in in the year ahead that you will know, that you know, that you know every step you take is ordered of the Lord.

Every word you speak is ordered of the Lord. Every contract you submit is ordered of the Lord. Hallelujah. Not only did Paul and Silas' prison doors open, but every prison door in that facility opened that night, at that moment, at midnight. That's what happened at midnight last night. The doors began to open, and so I'm decreeing and declaring and releasing a season of open doors. There will be no shut doors before you, but when you come into it, you're going to begin seeing those doors swing wide open in opportunity. Get ready. He's doing that and there's new doors opening. There are new opportunities opening. There are new God connections opening. You are one or two, possibly five connections away from that thing that you've been believing God for, and I call those connections to come. It's a covenant agreement today in Jesus name and nothing will hold you back from what God is doing, because

Lynette Dutton

He is doing a new thing, Beloved. Forget the former things. Don't mention or remind Him of the past any longer. When you pray, don't pray to remember how it used to be. He's doing a new thing. Don't even remember the old.

God has said old thing is not even your testimony any longer. Your testimony is the new thing He's doing today. He's not the thing He did 20 years ago. The testimony of Jesus Christ is what He's doing today. He said quit holding onto the old testimony. We're not ready to have a new testimony, but He is ready to give you a new miracle. He's ready to unleash a new thing in your life today. I sense right now that there is a supernatural thing happening in people's finances right now. It's supernatural, it's divine and don't question it when it comes. Don't question because people are going to begin writing bigger checks. The thing that you invented, the idea or book that you had that you've been struggling to get into production, that is a million-dollar thing that's causing the wealth transfer to come to you today, in Jesus' name. The wealth of the wicked is laid up for the just. There are even going to be people that you don't even think are worthy to submit money to you that are going to begin submitting money to you. There will be drug dealers. There will be people that have had crooked business ways. There will be people that are straight up heathens, and they don't know the word of God. But God is not allowing them to sleep until they start sowing money into your ministry, business, and into your life. They're going to come and they're going to sign the contracts. There are going to be secular contracts that come and are signed with your Christian company, because of your integrity, character, but most of all because God said so. God said, "It's your season. It's your time. It's your season. It's your day of short time. This is your year, Beloved. This is your year."

As you begin fine tuning your ear to the Spirit, as you start working the nine gifts of the Spirit into your life and into your business, as you start pursuing God's way above man's way, and as you start totally depending on him, He will supernaturally lining things up for you. I receive that for myself. I said, yes, God, me too Jesus. He's going to supernaturally and divinely orchestrate these things so fast. Amos 9 in the Message Bible says, "So fast, it's going to make your head spin." There's a head spinning anointing that is coming into your life, ministry, and into your business because things are going to start happening. The connections, the calls, the contracts, and the commissions are coming so quickly, it's going to make your head spin. I even see new facilities, new buildings, new properties. There are some things that have been on your heart and you say, God, am I going to have to let go of the old to purchase the new? He says, "No, it doesn't have to be either or, an *also* anointing is coming, and you don't have to leave one thing to walk into a new thing." God is putting the right structures, kingdom system, and the right laborers around you to help you do what you've been doing. This thing will begin to happen so supernaturally. Don't to try to wrap the natural mind around it. That's why we need the renewing of our minds because our natural mind is not going to be able to wrap around these spiritual things.

Business is a spiritual thing. Making money is a spiritual thing. Transactions are a spiritual thing. Relationships are a spiritual thing. He says, if you go into business, go like my priests go into ministry. Go in with the mindset that it's a worship, it's a spiritual thing. It's an act for God. It's me being Jesus to the world. He says, when you start taking that mindset into your business, into the secular realm, divine things begin to happen. He's flipping the switch today for some of you. You've just been walking in one thing, but now He's flipping the switch and the lights are coming on. Literally it's almost like you've walked into a vault except the lights were turned off, so you never saw the message, you never saw the gold around you.

For years I worked in banking. I was actually a vault teller in the year 2000, and we had excess money in lockboxes nobody could see by going in there. But if you opened the doors, there were stacks of cash in there because they thought the computer systems were crashing. But you know what? They didn't crash. We just had excess money. Likewise, when you walked into the dark, you didn't see anything, but God is flipping the switch for you today. Think of that opportunity you weren't even sure would make you the money you thought it might. You weren't sure but, God is flipping the switch and I see carts of money. He has opened the vault doors for you my brother and my sister. All He's asking for you to do is to be a giver, to be a good steward, and to walk in the Spirit of God. And so, follow His lead. He's the best leader, you might not be able to lead, but if you follow Holy Spirit, you just follow and seek after God. He will lead you every step.

He is flipping on the switch in that vault that you walked into in the last season, but you didn't even realize it because the lights weren't on. But He is illuminating and causing you the fresh revelation to tap into the wealth that is all already all around you, and you didn't even know it. There are millions stacking up all around you.

Prayer

I'm going to seal this word over your life. God, I ask that every prophetic word, every scripture, every word that you've given me for these men and women of God, these entrepreneurs, these ministers and the people that have been trying to figure out what you've called them to do… God, I ask right now that you seal it in their life and that you allow it to begin working today for them now in Jesus name. I thank you God, that it's going to bring forth much fruit. That seed is coming up to fruition and the harvest will be plenteous right now in Jesus' name, and I thank you God, that you're causing a spirit of acceleration and momentum to come upon everything that their hands touch, every idea, every strategy, every vision, every book that is inside them, the spirit of a finisher is upon them. God, I pray that they will finish everything that you've started. Lord, I ask that you heal these women of their past wounds and soul issues, and make them every bit whole. Bring them into their new season now. Holy Spirit, breathe upon this reader, in Jesus mighty name, Amen.

Isaiah 43:18-19 says, "Forget the former things to not dwell on the past. See, I am doing a new thing now that we're now is so important now. It springs up do you not perceive it." It's already done. Sisters, it's already done. And in 2 Corinthians 5:17, "Therefore, if any man be in Christ, he is a new creature. The old things are passed away and behold, all things are become new today." He's doing a new thing inside of you and I'm so excited. He's doing a new thing inside of your business. He's doing a new thing inside of your ministry. Most of all, he's doing a new thing inside of you and your mind. You're going to be able to take that territory that He has been preparing for you, that He's been telling you about, that He's been giving you cues and clues about. It's now! Say out loud, "It's mine now!" We always said it's your next, but it's your now. He's doing it now. Your next is now.

Questions for Reflection:

- What territory, region, or industry are you called to influence?
- What do you need to let go of so you can embrace the new God has for you?
- In what areas of your life, business, or ministry do you think God wants you to begin thinking and dreaming BIGGER?

Bio

Pastor Lynette Dutton, is one of the most sought-after women in North Carolina and across the country for incredible transforming teaching and story of life breakthroughs. She is co-pastor of The Epicenter Church and the Vice President of Dominion TV.

Lynette has her coaching certifications through the world-renowned Dream Releaser Coaching by Dr. Samuel Chand and The John Maxwell Team. Lynette has spent the last 25 years in leadership roles both in

Lynette Dutton

corporate America and in the church, giving her a unique perspective that she uses as a speaker, coach, and consultant.

Lynette considers herself to be very fortunate. Empowering others to achieve their dream is her life's pursuit and the heart of what makes her who she is. **Learn more about Lynette at lynettdutton.com**

It's A New Era

Jade Simmons

I truly believe we are not just in a new year or a new season, but we're entering a new era. I have several audacious prayers that will help you to excel in this new era. Before each prayer, I'm going to lay out what I feel like God has been revealing to me about entrepreneurship, about entrepreneurs, and about His people.

A Deeper Understanding of 'Epic'

My son, Jaden, has been learning how to skateboard and he's been using this word that's a part of skateboard culture. Epic is the word. He sees someone else doing a really amazing trick and he'll say, "Man, that was epic!" I'm listening to how that word has become so overused. When I hear a word being used a lot, I get curious because we know that God is the creator of all things, which means that all the words are His. So, I automatically want to go back and find out what that word really meant, what God intended us to understand. So, when the teenage crowd says 'epic', they mean that something's really big, really cool, or awesome. When I looked up the word 'epic', here's what I discovered. Epic is firstly a long poem. Typically, one derived from ancient oral tradition that narrates the deeds and adventures of heroic or legendary figures, or the history of a nation. (as taken from Webster's Dictionary).

Listen when I say that the year ahead is going to be epic! This is the year that God writes the part of *your* story that goes down in history. This is the year that sets you up to become one of the great adventurers of all time - one of the heroes, one of the legendary figures. You're going to be a part of leading nations into historical seasons and periods. This season is going to be about writing your story, but not until you commit to carrying out His story. You see, we are on this earth to finish God's work, (John 4:34-38) and we are privileged, honored, and humbled by the fact that He would use us to even write a chapter of history. You do know He doesn't really need us, right?

He doesn't really need us, but He has given us the privilege to be a part of this journey. So, we need to be excited. We need to have our hearts open. If you've never dreamt big enough to think that your life would be an epic, a long poem that people recite when they talk about the life you've lived... Start. Dreaming. Bigger. It's time for us to commit to some expansion. I always tell women I work with they need to get their hearts some stretch pants, because what God is going to do will stretch you. In order for you to believe that you're worthy of the big stuff that He's going to have you do, you'll need to be stretched.

Not a New Season, but a New Era

This is also not a season where you need to be found fumbling. You can't pray for all this breakthrough and then just leave the dream alone. We often just wait for God to "make it happen." What we're supposed to be doing is going back and constantly preparing and positioning. I keep saying the word 'season,' but I want to switch now because what I want to really pray about is this new era. I want you to have New Era Expectations. We're going to elevate just for a little bit now *above* the idea of seasons. Seasons are temporary periods with specific purposes attached to them. We're always living in seasons; we live cyclical lives. But let's decide not to get addicted to a season, because seasons are there to serve a purpose which is to elevate you into your next level, and ultimately, into your next era. Eras don't happen every year, but I believe that *this* year is when we're going to get the opportunity to decide to move into our new era. This is especially for those of you who did not give up at the end of last year. You got it right and did the right things. You held fast where your faith was concerned. Those of you who did that, who held on, you're going to see greater and faster rewards. This is going to be a season and an era of velocity.

Some of you think that counts you out because you gave up a few months ago. You gave up last summer. Some of you made it until a certain point and then realized nothing you wanted was happening, so you gave up. You figured, maybe I didn't see things right. Maybe I didn't hear correctly. Let me tell you, you still have time to get in position and to get into a position of faith. 2 Corinthians 5:17 says, "Therefore, if anyone is in Christ, the new creation has come, the old has gone, the new is here. I'm going to pray right now for forgetfulness of last year's failures.

Prayer for Forgetfulness of Past Failures

Father God, I thank you right now that you have the power to wipe the slate clean, including the slate of our brains, our souls, and our hearts that want desperately to hold on to past failures and past mistakes. We relinquish those things to you right now. We will not hold on to our past as idols. We will not lift those things up, not even our successes, Father. Make us even be forgetful while we're grateful for them. Make us be forgetful of the things we even got right, including the strategies we used last year, because You are doing a new thing, God. That means the stuff that brought in breakthrough last year might be old news. So, I thank you, Father God, that you're giving us new systems, new modes of operations, and new mindsets so that we can do things differently.

Do not let us cling to the past, Father. I thank You that You are a God who makes all things new and that begins with each one of us. So, Father, help us be forgetful. Help us be forgetful of the people who hurt us last year. Do not let us drag that hurt and pain around with us all year Father. Today is a new day. We will rejoice in it. We will be glad in it, Father God. I thank you that you will help us forget the strategies that failed us, the launches that fell flat, the products that didn't sell. Help us Father God to forget all of those things. Help us to forget them. Let them be tossed into a sea of forgetfulness just like you do with our sins. Speaking of sins Father, help us forget the times we fell short, felt like we shamed you, or thought you were embarrassed by our words, our behavior, or our thoughts. Help us forget the times we were jealous and envious over those who had greater success in business than we did, Father. Forgive us for the time that we dared to compare ourselves with others, because that in and of itself, was disrespectful to you. Father, we repent of comparison because we know that with you, we have a God who has broken the mold. Every time you created each one of us, you broke that mold, Father, and declared that there would be no one else like us. Father, we ask you to allow us to forget what didn't work and to give us hope for what's coming.

My Soul Thirsts for You

Psalm 63: 1 says, *"Oh God, you are my God."* This is my man David speaking, and he says, *"Early, will I seek to you. My soul thirsts for you, my flesh longs for you in a dry and thirsty land."* We have to be thirsty this year. I know the word thirsty has gotten a bad connotation of being desperate, but we have to decide to be thirsty on purpose for God. Not thirsty for people, not thirsty for networking and connections, for success, or even recognition. We have to decide to be thirsty for Him. I read something on the website, Bible Hub. One of the authors, named R. Glover, talks about Psalm 63 where David is saying that he's going to seek God and that his soul thirsted for him. He says,

"In that prayer with David, life would lose its light, it's worth, it's meaning, all of its delight and all of its joy without God. Ask David whether man could do without God, and he would tell you that without God, this world is just lodging, like it's just shelter. But with God, it is home. It's really home. It's a very different thing. He would tell you that without God, there is no sunlight in the world, no meaning and history, no hope for humanity, no prospect. Without our God, there was nothing to enfranchise the soul, to emancipate it, to enlarge it. But with God's presence, life has dignity. It develops its forces and with Him it is secure. David would tell you that without God, the soul has no model on which to mold its life. No motive with which to animate itself in conflict or no quiet resting place. David, above all things, wants God. He wants God in the sense of wanting God's presence, God's love, God's protection, and God's vindication. He wants to be the person who vindicates God; who stands up for God."

Whatever you want needs to take a back seat to wanting God. Whatever you're going after needs to take a back seat to going after God. I am going to pray here for God to give you a thirsty soul, one that is rarely quenched. It doesn't mean you're going to be left wanting, but you're going to be left with an intensity in your spirit that requires you to seek Him not just once a week, on Sundays and Wednesdays, or in 15 minutes of quiet time. But it's going to require you now to surrender most of your time to the act and the art of seeking Him.

Prayer for a Thirsty Soul

Father God, we just ask you to give us a thirsty soul. We ask you to expand the capacity, the containment possibilities of our soul, Father. If we've come to you before with a glass, Father, we just exchange it now for a pitcher. If we came to you with a pitcher Father, now we exchange it for a tub. If we came to you with a tub, Father God, we just ask you to exchange it for an ocean. Father, make it so every time we think we're full, we realize we are empty. It doesn't mean that we're going to feel like we are without you, but every time we get more of you, we're going to be greedy. Father, we're going to want even more than we had. Father, when we look back on the last year and thought we were doing something and thought we were seeking you, Father let it now look small in our eyes.

Let us increase our time with you, Father. Take us out of the daily stale habits of giving you 15 minutes of drive by service. Father, let us become dedicated to the process of worshipping you. I ask you, Father, to make us hunger for your word like never before. Make us be okay with the inspiration we get from man and okay with the great books that have been written, but make us only be satisfied in completion when we turn to you. Father let us decide that you will be our first source of inspiration, so that we will seek you like David said early in the morning. Get our lazy butts out of bed. Father light a fire under all of us and help us to realize that it is time for us to wake up and that once we wake up and open our eyes, you will then allow us to see new things.

Father, it's been cloudy for some of us. We felt blind last year so I thank you for new vision. Go ahead and give us new eyes in the year ahead. We know that nine is the number of birthing, so I thank you Father, that whatever we're designed to birth in this season, whatever we've been laboring hard for in those last few months Father, they will come into fruition right now. I thank you that the wheels are turning, the doors are opening, meetings are being had that we don't even know about. We're not going to focus on the doors. We're not going to focus on the breakthrough to business success. We're going to focus on you because you're going to make us thirstier than ever for you. Father, I ask that you allow that thirst to only be quenched by your presence.

Don't let us start off thirsty for you and then be satisfied for the breakthrough that you give us. Don't let us start out hungry for you and then be easily satisfied for recognition that man wants to give us Father. Make it be so that the thirst can only go in one direction. The quenching can only come from one direction. We pray all of that in your holy name. In Jesus' name, we pray. Amen.

Breakthrough is the New Black

I've been hearing this phrase in my head; *breakthrough is the new black*. We always talk about what new color is the new black meaning which current popular color is going to become the staple. We've said pink is the new black, orange is the new black, navy is the new black, etc. I declare that Breakthrough is the new black. Breakthrough is about to become your staple. You're about to wear breakthrough every day. You're about to experience daily breakthrough. You're going to pray now for breakthrough to become your mode of operation. Now, first what I have to do is redefine breakthrough for you. The commercial world, the ministry world, and the corporate world have all hijacked the word breakthrough. Whenever you read about breakthrough in the Bible, it's rarely breaking through to something, or some mode of success. And we love to think of it that way. But the first breakthrough is always breaking through *to* God. He wants your business to have success, not just so that you can get the new car that you have your eye on. It's so that when people see your success, they have to ask you what happened. And you have to describe to them what breakthrough really is. In response, you're going to say, don't look at this new car. Don't look at this new house, don't look at the numbers on my bottom line in my business, but look at my heart and soul and see that I've been thirsting like never before for God. Because 100% of my attention has gone to Him, He has tended to everything He has given me.

In this new era, your ideal client is God Himself. He's your ideal client because if you get it right with Him, He's going to handle everything. How many of you need help in your back office today? How many of you need systems, team members, or back office help? Guess what. Get it right with God, your ideal client. He'll work on your back office for you. We all have very different skills and gifts, but there's one anointing that each and every single one of us has and no one of us has more than the other, and that is the anointing to minister to God. We have all been called to minister to God.

What would happen if 100% of our focus went on ministering to God versus just focusing on ministering out of what God has given you, meaning ministering to people. So, my prayer for myself, and I'm going to make it your prayer as well, is to be focused on ministering to God. Using your anointing to worship Him, to lavish Him with more praise, to decide to have more connection with Him than ever before. Then, he's going to get the glory because your attention is on Him. He's going to take care of your business. If you want direction, minister to the Lord.

In Acts 13: 2, while they were ministering to the Lord and fasting, the Holy Spirit said set apart for me Barnabas and Saul for the work to which I have called them. We're talking about the time of all the great apostles. They needed direction. How many of you keep saying, God, I just need direction? Give me direction, give me clarity. I just imagine Him up there going, well, minister to me. Minister to me so that my Holy Spirit can speak to you. If you're looking for new strategy different from the stuff you tried last year that fell flat, stop asking for new strategy, stop asking for new directives. Get on your knees and say, God, I'm not even asking you for strategy. I'm just going to minister to you now and I know that if I minister to you, you're going to tell me what I need to know and what you need me to do. What you need me to do right now and what you need me to do later. We must remember that if we focus on ministering to Him first in this season, then we're going to have all the directives we need.

Exodus 33, that's Moses. What I love about Moses is that he spoke to God face to face. Scripture tells us the Lord used to speak to Moses face to face just as a man speaks to his friend. The real translation of face to face means mouth to mouth. It means that when Moses communicated to God, God was resuscitating him, breathing into his mouth. Inspiration really means God breathed. God breathed into Moses. If you want true inspiration, decide in this season to be like Moses.

A Prayer for Breakthrough to Him

Father God, I ask You to make us like Moses. Give us the same relationship. We are ready now, not just to speedily pray to You, Father. We're not even satisfied with getting in our prayer closet and just wailing and crying. We want even more than the ugly cry in this season. We want to hear from You directly. We want to breathe in and know that we're breathing You in and breathing You out on the people that You have given us. Father, we are sick and tired of our own wisdom, our own inspiration, our own systems, and our own knowledge. Father, shut our mouths when we start saying we have all the answers and that if the world just did it like we did it, they would be blessed. That's a lie from the pit of hell, Father. I thank You that we only want to give Your strategy to the world.

Father, break our strategies down. Give us divine strategy. Father, I thank you that this is a new era where you're going to be speaking to us face to face. Just as man speaks to his friend, we want to speak to You. We ask you Father to put breakthrough for our business, our family, and our home as secondary. Father, help us make our number one breakthrough be to You. We know if we make You our ideal client in this season, we will have broken through to the most important source we can have, and that breakthrough will unleash whatever we need to carry us into this new era.

A New Era of Expectancy

I want to end by talking to you about new era expectancy. I want you to expect different things than you expected last year. A really great friend of mine said to me, "Jade you know, I'm looking around and everybody's out there talking about their strategy. They've got all of their quarters planned out, all their months planned out, and they're making their vision boards." Then she said, "I don't want to do any of that stuff. I just don't feel led in this season to plan everything to a T." She and I are both avid planners, and we love to write everything down and plot everything out. She asked me, "Am I being a slacker? I feel like I'm slacking a little bit." I understand that feeling, but I asked her this one question. I said, listen, when you look back at the biggest breakthroughs you've had this past year, did they come from your master planning or did they come from surrendering to the master? I'll ask you this time: Did the best breakthroughs you had last year come from your master planning or did they come from surrendering to the master?

I'm going to go ahead and guess that it is the latter. That's what my friend admitted. When I looked back at it, that one question sums it up. If you can trace your biggest breakthroughs back to surrendering everything you know, everything you usually do to the Master, why would you change that up now? Am I saying not to plan? Am I saying don't have a strategy? No, just be loose enough with it to allow God to move. Write your stuff down, but do not marry it. Write it down and surrender it immediately. Write your dreams down and sacrifice them on an altar back to God immediately. Write everything you want, all your desires and surrender them immediately to God himself. This is a year of entering a new era. You can expect daily downloads with specific directives. When you minister directly to God 100% of the time, He will tell you what you need to know. This is a new era.

Prayer for a New Era

Father God, we thank you for a new era of expectation. We can and will expect more of you, Father God, because we're ready to receive more of you. We can expect your higher expectations on us. You want more from us. How dare we ask you for more and not sign up to give more emotionally, physically, and professionally? Father, help us work harder and smarter in this upcoming season. Help us give more and be more diligent. Help us to donate time and give more money. We can't dare ask you for breakthrough in our income and then be stingy on our side of the table. Father God, I thank you for a new type of heightened awareness. You are a God of detail. We saw you build the temple. We saw you give directions for Nehemiah's wall.

We know that you must then have those same direction for us. You directed Jesus' steps, you directed Paul's travels. Why wouldn't you direct us? Those of us who travel for business, we will not say yes to everything because we're hungry for money, or hungry for direction, or hungry to be able to say, I have a bunch of stuff on my calendar. We will only say yes to the places that God has called us to go. Some of you will be turning down engagements in this new era, because it is that kind of season. You're going to decide you want to be where God wants you to be more than you want to be where you want to go.

Father God, give us the anointing to listen in real time. We will not keep doing what we want to do because it looks good and feels good. But give us the intent, Father, to follow you like quick lightning. Help our amens turn into action. Help us go from inspiration straight to implementation. Let us be quick with our obedience, Father. Show us the patterns that you have been using in our lives. Do I need a vision board, Father? Do I need to plan it out? Do I need to make a blueprint? Father, if that's not the case, then you give us the divine strategy. You give us the breakthrough blueprint. Father, let us follow your voice more than any other minister's, more than any other coach, and more than any other guru.

Let your voice get first position in our mind's eye, in our brain, and in our inner ear. Father God, we pray for a clear blueprint and new templates made just for us. Father, we thank you that you've broken the mold with us. So do not let us begin to copy, to be copycats, or try on other people's skin for size because we know it will not fit. I thank you Father that you're going to refine us and recalibrate us on the go. We're not going to spend whole seasons preparing and positioning because this is a fast season that's going to move with velocity. Father, give us quick redirects. Give us the obedience that is quick. Give us fast obedience. Give us upgrades on the go. I thank you that you are adding some bells and whistles to my make and model. Father God, you're giving us a faster, better drive, a smoother ride in this season. You're upgrading us with higher technology in our person and in our business. Let them hear ticking time bombs in their ears. Give them the "as soon as" anointing Father. As soon as they hear your words, they will move. As soon as they know your direction, they will go. As soon as they hear the directive, they will speak into the lives of who they are called to speak to. We thank you for fast obedience. Lastly, I thank you that the foundations that were good that we laid down in the past cannot be dug up. We will not go in reverse in this season. If we have beaten depression before, we're not carrying it into this near era. If we have beaten anxiety or indecision before, we're not carrying it with us.

Those foundations that have been laid are solid. They will not be dug up. Neither will old dusty bones be dug up, Father. Everything that we buried, killed, and slayed in the past will stay dead. I thank you right now for a new day. I thank you that you are a God of the new and that change is a part of your M.O. We will not stay stuck in old places. We will not be people glued to an old year, old habits, old modes of operations, and old mindsets. I thank you that you are making all things new in this era. Father, we will choose you. We will choose you this day. As things begin to be separated in this year, as the wheat and the chaff are distinguished, we thank you that we are wheat. We thank you that we will be found on the right side of the line. I thank you for that. In your holy name, we pray, Amen.

Questions for Reflection:

- What do you feel like God is saying to you when you read, "Not a new a season but a new era?"

- What did forgetfulness of your past failures free you up to do more of?

- If our first breakthrough is always breaking through *to* God, how would you like to go deeper in your relationship with Him.

Bio

Jade Simmons is a powerhouse keynote speaker, concert pianist, and minister. She is also a coach to visionary women of faith who are looking to be bolder in this next era. Jade is also the author of *Audacious Prayers for World Changers – How to Live and Pray Out Loud.* **Learn more about Jade at jadesimmons.com**

Dare to Believe…

You Are
Filled and
Growing Beyond
Your Current Capacity!

Fill My Cup

Lana Hunter

My prayer is for us to ask God to fill our cups until we want no more. Fill our cups until we are no longer satisfied with church as usual. Fill our cups until we experience Him at levels we haven't experienced before.

Fill my cup Lord, I lift it up, Lord, come and quench this thirsting in my soul. Bread from heaven feed me till I want no more. Here's my cup, fill it up and make me whole.

The words to this song are so simple, yet so powerful. But what do they really mean? What does it mean to be filled? It means, "to occupy, take up or have the capacity for more."

And what does this have to do with you being an entrepreneur or whatever you might be? Well, for me, I see the cup as being a business. It may be a business, a book, a gift, or whatever that thing is that God has entrusted you with. God gave you that thing. But the question that we need to ask is, are we lifting it up to Him and asking Him to fill it up, or are we trying to do it ourselves? Are we doing what everyone else is doing, doing what we learned from someone else? Perhaps we do whatever's trending. Or maybe we just do what we've done before because it worked. But we haven't asked God about what He might want to do through us now. We haven't asked Him to breathe on what's in our cup. We haven't asked for directions. We're just doing. We're just going on autopilot. So today we're going to ask God to fill our cups with fresh oil. God wants to fill our cup with good things. Psalms 103:5 says,

> *"Who satisfies your mouth with good things, so that your youth is renewed like the eagle's."*

You might be asking, so how do I get my cup filled? I think it's a daily process for sure, a regular asking. It's something that you're never going to get so much of that there's no capacity for more. There's always room for more. I'm so greedy that even when my cup is full and it spills over, I want to share the overflow. So, don't worry if you think that your cup is so full and you're good. No, I think our cups need to be filled daily. So how do I get my cup filled? The filling comes from Him giving us divine directions and downloads. He's still providing fresh ideas. There seems to be nothing new under the sun, but I know that God hasn't run out of ideas. He created us, and we are creative beings.

I think about when I started doing brunch events over ten years ago. There weren't a whole lot of brunches or women's empowerment events then, but now it seems as though everyone is doing a similar type of event. Someone said to a friend of mine about my brunch events, "Everybody's doing brunches now." That same friend reminded me that, yes, everyone might be doing a brunch, but they're not doing it at the level or having the impact that you are having. So, don't forget that. Don't get caught up with who's doing what you're doing, because God is giving you divine direction and downloads about how to do the very thing that He's putting your hand.

The filling comes when you seek His face and not just His hands. Think about your why. Why are you wanting to do what you're doing? If it's for money, you'll always be chasing money. If it's to serve, then guess what? Money's going to chase you. You don't have to sell water to a thirsty person. You just don't. He'll see what you have and come to you to get that need filled.

The filling comes when we spend time with Him, and He gives us witty ideas and inventions that might be imitated but can't be duplicated. Your anointing cannot be duplicated. There's room for you, there's an audience for you. There are things that you can do that no one else can do. And sometimes the things that come so naturally to you, you might think everybody can also do the same thing. That's not necessarily the case. It comes so easily because that's your cup, that's what God has given you. Remember Moses and the staff that became a serpent? Well the magicians did the same thing. Yet, Moses' serpent ate up the others.

The next line says, *"Come and quench this thirsting in my soul."* How does He quench our thirst as it relates to business? He provides fresh ideas for your business, your book, or whatever your cup is. He gives you your daily bread. So be sure to stay focused on pleasing Him and not pleasing people. Worrying about pleasing people is like putting God in the back seat, and if He's in the back seat, He can't be the pilot. He's the one that's driving, not us. He should be the beginning, the middle, and the end of everything we do. So, the quenching also comes from when we pray bold and audacious prayers. We're not praying "if this happens," we're speaking those things into existence. The word says faith is the substance of things hoped for and the evidence of things not yet seen. But see it as if it's already done. In the end, we see what we say. So, declare that it is so, because God has said so.

How has He done that? He said it in His word. His word says we are the head and not the tail. That means that you are leading. You are not following. His word says that we are lenders and not borrowers. His word says we might walk through the shadow of death and not be afraid. So, when we go through situations that try to take us out, we come out better than when we went in. Listen, when the Israelites went through their 400-year trial they came out of Egypt with enemies that were favorably disposed towards them. They left bondage filthy rich. It doesn't make sense in the natural, but that's God. God takes the foolish things to confound the wise. He takes the things that seem so quirky to us in the physical and makes that thing a thing. Whoa, that only could be God!

"Bread from heaven, feed me till I want no more."

We know God is our bread from heaven and we are eating His word. Are you hungry? Are you eating His word? If not, what are you feeding on? Social media? Conferences? Are you running to receive a prophetic word rather than spending time in the word? What are you feeding yourself? You might need to stop feeding yourself. Can you miss a meal or two sometime other than at the beginning of the year, so that we don't become hungry for anything other than God? Maybe we're full, eating the lies that people are telling us. Lies like,

- Everybody is doing that.
- Everyone has a book.
- Everyone's a coach or speaker.
- Everyone is doing brunches.
- Everyone is a financial coach.
- Nobody does it like that, so it will never work.
- You can't be that different.
- The market is too saturated.

Reject the lies and stop eating the fears of others. Everyone shouldn't be able to speak over and into your life. You can't share your dreams with everyone. Remember when God told Noah to build an ark when no one had seen a ship or flooding before? What if he'd listened to the crowd? God told Moses to hold his staff over the water so the people could cross over on dry land. Nobody had ever done that before either, and it seemed like the most ridiculous thing in the natural. But guess what? Millions of people came through on that dry land, because Moses ate what God fed him. I'm sure someone was like, listen, that's not going to work. The laws of physics and nature don't work like that. But what if he'd listened to them? We can't listen to the opinions of people when our God told us to do the thing that seems foolish in the natural. Elijah told a king to get ready for rain when it hadn't rained in 3 years. How bold is that!!

People will tell you, no one's doing that. That can't be done. You are trying to be too new and too radical. Let them know... You're not my bread of heaven. I'm going to listen to the bread of heaven and let Him feed me. Remember, God doesn't always do the thing we're expecting Him to do in the manner in which we expect Him to do it. Sometimes we get disappointed. But guess what? I want it done. So, I'm going to trust the one that I know can do it, and I encourage you to do the same. He is God, and He could do whatever He wants, but if we eat what He has prepared for us, we will never go hungry.

Psalms 107:9 tells us that. It says, He satisfies the thirsty and fills the hungry with good things. I encourage you today to give your gift, your business, your talent, whatever it is that you have that you've been handling yourself back to God. Starting now. Ask God, take this back and let me take my hands off of it so you can come in and be glorified. Let's pray.

Prayer

God, I just thank you that you are the bread of heaven. I appreciate that you satisfy the hungry and those that are thirsty. God, I thank you that we recognize we are nothing without you, but with you, we can do all things. Our businesses can be trendsetters. Our companies can make a global impact for you. God our integrity goes before us which is really yours since we are your children. Father, I thank you that people know us and are speaking our names when we're not in those circles or rooms. God, I thank you that you are setting it up that we just have to walk after you, thirst after you, and you will guide our steps. You will bring the contacts and contracts. You will bring the clients God, and you will give us the right publishers and partners that we need. God, we are thankful that you have brought us this far on this journey. We thank you, for all the lessons learned and strides we've made. We thank you God for preparing and positioning us for divine appointments. We thank you Lord that prayer helps us to discern our next steps which are revealed as we spend time with you filling us. God, we no longer will look to the left, or to the right, or to anyone other than you. We won't start our days without asking Lord, what's next? What conversation do I need to have today? Who do I reach out to? Who can I be a blessing to? Help me to write this blog and it change the life of the people reading it. Let this post impact the people that are reading it and let it minister to them just at the place of need. God, we know you will give us what we need when we spend time in your presence. We thank you, Lord God, that in your presence we can find everything we need. God take us to places we haven't imagined and do things that don't currently exist. God, we thank you for opening those doors. Your word says that you can do more than we can ask, think, or imagine, and we're pretty imaginative people. But you are God, the creator of the universe God. The God that sits high and looks low. Lord, we thank you because we know that if we can imagine a thing you can do even more than that. We thank you God, that as we seek you, opportunities will find us. We thank you, God, that you can change the heart of any Pharaoh today. We thank you God, that we don't have to beg for business. We have the necessary books. We can speak into the lives of the people that need to hear what we have to say. Father, we thank you. God, we will not take matters into our own hands or try to fill our own cup. God, we are saying to you today, now and always, fill my cup Lord. We lift it up God, come and quench the thirsting in my soul. Bread of heaven, feed us until we want no more. Every day we give our gifts, talents, abilities, even our flaws, hiccups, or mistakes to you. God have your way. God create in us clean hearts and a new way of thinking. We want the mind of Christ, so that our minds line up to the word and the will of God. Let our mouth, our hearts, and our whole being be in alignment with your word. Less of us and more of you God. Let us hunger and thirst for you. God, we thank you. We honor you. We lift our cups up to you, and we give back to you what you first gave us. We thank you. Make us good stewards of our cups. Let us handle it properly as we operate in and with integrity. Let us serve in love. Let our business and our services be impeccable. People will look for us and they won't have to look far. They will find us because we are visible. We are doing the thing you've created us to do. We're not doing it in a silo or in silence. We are doing the things that you've called us to do in the marketplace, and as a result, lives are being changed. Atmospheres are being shifted. People are being set free. God, we thank you, and we honor you in Jesus name, and so shall it be. Amen.

Questions for Reflection:
- How are you currently filling your cup?
- What's working? What can you do more or less of?
- What or who gets impacted when your cup is not full?
- What are 3 things you can do daily to keep your cup full?

Bio

Lana Hunter is the go-to strategist for influencers as well as small businesses. She has a natural ability to create, implement, and execute processes and operations, as well as the keenness needed to run events of all sizes seamlessly. Her corporate career spans 20 plus years doing just that for many fortune 500 companies.

After spending years developing and executing strategies that aim to improve the client experiences for many notable companies, Lana took a courageous leap and started a business. Her passion for serving, planning, and creating great client experiences led her to start this business. Her event planning and business administration skills create amazing client experiences that impact bottom lines.

A native of the beautiful island of Nassau in the Bahamas, Lana loves and lives colorfully. Now calling Grand Prairie, TX home, you can find her serving in her community, planning or hosting the next most fabulous event, or simply at home with her family and friends. **Learn more about Lana at sundressbrunch.com**

Go Beyond

Kelli K. Fisher

When I look back over my life, I am thankful to the Lord for where He's brought me from and marvel at how important my walk with Him has become. Like the old saying goes, "I'm not where I want to be, but I'm not where I used to be." I've finally arrived at a point in my life where there is nothing more important than my relationship with God, and come what may, I'm sold out to see what the end is going to be. Putting my full hand (not just a couple of fingers anymore) in His hand and leaning in to the guiding of the Holy Spirit to order my steps in business and life has been scary at times because it pushes me to rely on Him. It has also been reassuring that even when I hear God's voice urging me to do something or go somewhere, I know He will never leave me or forsake me and, in the end, it will be for His and *my* good.

So, as I sit here at the computer sipping my Chai tea latte from my very favorite mug, before I share even one thought, I'd like to just begin in prayer. Shall we? I'm so grateful right now.

Thank you, God. Thank you, Jesus, for allowing us to see another second, minute, hour, month, and year. Hallelujah. Lord we just thank you for the growth we've had, whether it's overcoming obstacles just yesterday or You carrying us through times that we just couldn't see our way out. Thank you, God, for placing in us this desire to seek You in such a way that we would want to read this devotional book and learn more about You, and even hear Your voice in a way that we can apply to our own life's journey. I thank You Lord for each and every person who will eventually be led to pick up this book and I ask, God, that You would meet them right where they are. Help them to feel Your touch and Your abundant love that cannot be compared to anything or anyone else. Speak Lord as only You can. We give You all the glory, all the honor and all the praise for who You are and who You've been to each one of us. We seek Your face God and Your understanding of the plan that You have set before us. When You created us, You stepped back in wonder and said that it was good. We are equipped with everything we need if we would only rely fully and completely on You. Help us God to lean on You and not to our own understanding. In all our ways we want to acknowledge You, knowing that You will direct our paths. We thank you for growth. God, we thank you for all that you're doing in our lives. For every entrepreneur, every business owner, God, every person who is thinking of starting a business, every person whom you've planted something in their hearts to do for Your glory, for Your kingdom, bless them and order their steps.

God, we just thank you for gathering us here at this moment at this appointed time. We just praise you God. We magnify your name! Lord, we could never have enough words to adequately praise You for what you've done for us, Lord. If we had 10,000 tongues it still wouldn't be enough. But we thank You God for never leaving or forsaking us. We thank You for hand selecting each person who will read this and knitting us together to encourage one another. You're so worthy God, and everything You do is on purpose. We give you the highest praise and ask that You go before me and set the atmosphere. Not my will but thy will be done. In Jesus mighty and matchless name, Amen and Amen.

I had to get that out because I'm just so thankful. And like I said, I could go on forever as to what that means to me and what God has done. He has gotten me through small things and huge things. Times when I literally thought that I couldn't go any further, times when my back was pressed against the wall and He came through. He continues to come through for me and I love Him today for that. I'm sure you have your own testimonies as well that would make for good conversation full of amazement and eventually a collective run of rejoicing around the room.

Kelli K. Fisher

As some of you may know I am a certified life and relationship coach. I'm a business owner, a speaker, and I co-authored another book called Relationship DUOvers. Many of you might know me as one half of The Matchmaking Duo. Melissa Nixon and I are connected in many ways. One of which is, along with my business partner, being prayer partners for many years as sister friends and entrepreneurs, praying for each other personally and believing God to move in our respective companies. We all often say this journey of an entrepreneur is not for the faint of heart. Sidebar, if you don't have a prayer partner that you can pray with and believe God together for your wildest dreams, start praying for God to send you one, or a few for that matter. Your circle of support and influence can make such a huge impact on your momentum or lack of.

As an entrepreneur, there are so many goals I still have yet to achieve and I'm believing God they will come to fruition. But to people on the outside looking in or those just starting out with their own business, many may see the present outcome of my many years of hard work. I've been blessed to be featured on various national media outlets and stages along the way from television networks, women's conferences, radio segments, churches, and even our own podcast as either a subject matter expert or encourager in an area of life I've overcome. One of my favorite quotes by Steve Jobs I find so appropriate for this entrepreneurial journey says, "If you really look closely, most overnight successes took a long time." So funny and so true. An average of 7-10 years to be exact, and these seemingly overnight successes usually have a back story attached comprised of an incomparable amount of determination, grit, and being faced with and overcoming tremendous obstacles, but that's another story. The point is that we focus on the end result often, not knowing the backstory which can fool us into thinking that we're somehow different and success is unattainable; it seems so far away.

So, God led me to share a small portion of my back story in hopes that it will encourage you. In addition to what you see in front of you today, I am a divorced solo parent of three beautiful daughters, now ages 14,

13, and 9, and I'm a servant of God. A lot of times we're not able to always put our faith in the forefront when we're working in a business setting or in corporate America. But yes, I am a servant of God and I love the Lord and my heart is turned toward Him. I'm not perfect by any stretch of the imagination, but I've arrived at a point in my life where I continue to press my way to be closer to Him, to hear His voice, and follow His lead for my life. My life to date has consisted of so many faith leaps. And I'm not saying that to toot my own horn, but looking back, these faith leaps strengthened my relationship and trust in God more than I could've ever imagined, and each one has truly been a much needed segue to becoming an entrepreneur. As I prayed and asked God for a topic to share with you, He said, tell them to **Go Beyond**. At the time I wasn't sure how it would all tie in, but He then reminded me of some of the faith leaps that I've had to take in my life that took place prior to me arriving where I am today.

The first major faith leap that comes to mind is when one of my daughters was diagnosed with a rare form of cancer at age 4. We were going along living the life, or so we thought, and boom we were hit with a diagnosis of a mere 30% chance that she would live. We don't have enough time to adequately discuss how my relationship with God came to life during that time and how it went from going through the motions to igniting my faith into pure fire as we fought to keep her alive. Thankfully she's alive to one day tell her story. You can only imagine however as a mom how I eventually had to come face to face with the decision to either just go along with the motions and feelings of possible defeat or walk in faith, giving that situation completely to God, trusting Him no matter what the outcome would be. I eventually chose the latter, and from that experience realized that my relationship with God would need to be put into action even with my most precious decisions and commodities.

And so fast forward to a few more faith leaps. The second one was hearing the voice of God urging me to relocate to Charlotte, NC from New

Jersey after divorce with now 3 young daughters, (my youngest was just turning 2). This leap would require me to navigate in a completely new location as a new solo parent, with a new job, and knowing less than a handful of people in the area. Really God? But somehow in my spirit, I knew it was the right move for our peace and stability and I had to trust Him fully even though I wasn't quite sure how it all would turn out. I made the move and now more than 7 years into it, I still marvel at how amazing God's plan turned out. Wow. The lessons I've learned, the growth I've seen in myself and my daughters, and all that I've accomplished with God's help in this short time could be a book all on its own. God is so good!

I would say the last faith leaps that come to mind are the various decisions I've made for my daughters' wellbeing that many would say went against the grain. For instance, over time, I realized that each of my daughters had such different personalities and interests which meant unfortunately, although it wouldn't be comfortable for me, they needed to break up and attend different schools that best fit them. OMG. Really Lord? I started researching and God led me to great options, but they turned out to be 30 minutes away from me; one public, one private, one magnet. Yes Lord, ok. We started applying one at a time as God led, and I will say although it was and still is a huge sacrifice for me, each one was accepted and they are finally comfortable, thriving, and making their own way. Thank you, Jesus.

So, when God began speaking to me about starting a business, I look back and none of the faith leaps up to that point were comfortable. In fact, they were extremely uncomfortable and to others who couldn't see with spiritual eyes, it probably didn't make much "common sense." Every step required me to go past, **go beyond** my comfort zone and it still does to this day. And it's so funny, people would say to me, "Wow, I've seen you on TV. I've heard you on the radio. I've seen you as a keynote speaker, or as a guest on The Steve Harvey show and different places. That must be so amazing!" And it has been. But you know what?

If we go back, who was born knowing how to be comfortable on TV or do any of those things, right? All of it required a faith leap at one time or another. It required ***going beyond*** my comfort zone. Like everyone else before me, I was scared to death the first time, but where is our faith? God is reminding us to do it afraid and follow His lead, even when it's something you've never done. I've realized that this is a requirement to true success and living in the purpose that's been placed in you. Even now, when I see someone who is doing great things, my mind quickly goes to, "Wow, I wonder what they had to do to get there. Did they just fall into it? No. What risks did they have to take fully believing in nothing else but themselves and God? What was their turning point where they had to ***Go Beyond*** what they knew in their own strength and their own comprehension of what they could do, and launch forward anyway trusting wholeheartedly with no hesitation that God had their back and He was with them?"

Have you noticed that when God shows us His promises for us or plants something deep down in our soul that He wants us to do for His kingdom, He pretty much gives us what the end result is supposed to be? Then He presents us with an opportunity to take small steps along the way. So, the most important part is hearing His voice and just taking the step. The next thing I've noticed about this process of ***Going Beyond*** is that doing the things God has called us to do quite often is not something we feel we can do on our own or in our own strength. Have you noticed that? After all, if we could do it all on our own why do we need God? And how would we be assured of the magnitude of His power and love for us if we never allow Him the opportunity to show us?

Growing up, I watched my father go from being a teacher to eventually earning his doctorate degree in education, start and run an amazing magazine, teach himself the stock market, purchase real estate, and give back by establishing a support group for inner city children at his church. My mother had a very successful business for over 25 years that she started in the 80's. I can only imagine how often she had to ***Go Beyond*** during that initial time of even thinking to start her company. She was a girl who was born in a small town in Georgia, as 1 of 6 siblings with a high school education, and no formal training in entrepreneurship. When she retired, her company had grown to a multi-million-dollar business interfacing and meeting the needs of Fortune 100 companies across the country and the world. Look at God! They were both strong in their faith along the way, and I figured as I was writing this chapter, I would ask my mother if there was anything she could share with the readers about her experience as an entrepreneur of faith. She said, "You know, there will be times that you're frustrated or overwhelmed, but you'll realize that the issue is often that you're doing it in your own strength, and often what God asks us to do is not something we can achieve by ourselves. I often told God, this is His business and His reputation, not mine. Wherever He leads me I'll go."

Another thing to realize is that when you're birthing something new, it's not always going to be business as usual in our lives. We wish it could all fit into this neat square box with a bow, but anticipate that sacrifices will have to be made. I remember when God told me to co-author my book along with my business partner. My dynamics were different. As I mentioned, I was still working a new job, I had young children, and was in a new city. My youngest daughter was maybe 3 years old at this time, so the others were 8 and 9. So how would the book get done? After doing everything else throughout the day, I devoted a certain amount of time to writing. Sometimes 30 minutes, sometimes an hour, or even 2 hours at night when the children were off to sleep, or I would have meetings with my business partner or editor with a start time of 9 or 10 p.m. Was it easy? No. Crazy? Maybe. But in my mind, it was either that or come up with excuses as to why I couldn't get it done and believe me I had many valid excuses that I could safely rely on.

For you, the sacrifice might be something different given your circumstances like less sleep (definitely less sleep), or giving up a vacation, or time with friends, or to make time and additional resources to get things done. You might have to pick up the phone and call some people or email someone out of the blue that God tells you to connect with, which we've had to do plenty of times. You may even walk into some doors and join some circles that are not familiar. God might say, "You know what? I need you to join that circle. I need you to join that group. I need you to do something unconventional. No, these people don't even know you, but I'm telling you, I'm opening the door and I need you to walk in." Proverbs 18:16 says, "A man's gift opens doors for him and brings him before great men." That's one of my favorite scriptures that keeps me encouraged and reminds me at times like this that it might seem scary, but my gift has already opened the door. All I need to do is be obedient and show up. So, God equips us with what we need, and it allows us to *Go Beyond* what's comfortable and trust in Him.

Another verse that comes to mind is Ephesians 3:20-21, "Now to Him who is able to do exceedingly abundantly above all that we can ask or think according to the power that works in us." The Bible is talking about the power within that God has given us. Not just any power, but the power to be able to walk with boldness. Then it has to use not one, not two, but three adjectives to adequately explain how much God is able to do; exceedingly, abundantly, and above all. That means God can *Go Beyond* what we can actually ask, think, or even comprehend in our brains. So why are we limiting ourselves to only what we can humanly imagine? God is waiting for us to activate that power and put it into motion. 1 John 4:4 says, "Greater is He who is in us than he that is in the world." So, we're walking around with all of this power and God's saying that He will do exceedingly, abundantly above all. So, guess what? There's no need to be fearful. We're ready. We are equipped with whatever it is that He's given us to do.

Now that we've had a moment to see this from a Godly perspective, what plans do you have for your life or businesses that in hindsight might be based on your own strength today? I had to stop and think about this myself. We can have the best laid plans and just be so proud of ourselves, but let's stop and think again. Is what you have in mind God's plan? I mean, do you feel like you've **_Gone Beyond_**?

- Have you really stretched your mind to go beyond and tap into what God can do and not what we can do in our own strength?
- Are you selling yourself short?
- Are you operating strictly in your own power?

For example, maybe you're operating locally now, if we consult with God, would His plan be to expand? Do you have other skills or passions that you're not tapping into due to fear or not being assured how it will all turn out, but you know without a doubt that you can be a blessing in that area to someone else? Is fear of the unknown, or fear of not being "perfect," or having a past keeping you from going beyond to align your mind with all the greatness God has planted in you? 2 Timothy 1:7 says, "For God has not given us the spirit of fear, but of power, love, and a sound mind." Oh wow, there's that word *power* again. We have the power within that He has placed in each one of us. Maybe you're even still working for someone else and there's a position you know in your spirit you should be applying for, but you just can't imagine how it will all work out in your favor. Guess what? It's not for us to know. Take the first step and follow God's lead. Philippians 4:13 says, "I can do all things through Christ who strengthens us." So, let's remind ourselves of the God that we serve in our businesses and in our life as we move forward.

One last thing I should share is the revelation I've received recently from a verse I've heard probably hundreds of times over the years, but it has become more relevant to me in this season. For a long time, I was under the impression that because I had overcome several major obstacles and stepped out in faith many times that I was done. I learned my lesson. I've done my job. But God opened my eyes on this verse one day when I heard it again. Romans 1:17, "The righteousness of God is revealed from faith to faith. The righteous will live by faith." I heard this again and it hit me that not only are we *living* by faith, meaning ongoing, there are different levels of faith and many opportunities in our lifetime to experience it. So just because I trusted God for my daughter's healing, (or even more so had to decide that He would still be God if he chose not to) just because I took a leap of faith to relocate to a new state as a single parent miles away from my family, just because I forged ahead to start a business, or I wrote a book, I thought I was done! I thought, "Lord I've not only believed but I've activated my faith, I've learned valuable lessons along the way, and praise God now I've arrived at a whole new place of confidence, contentment, and fulfillment. To top it all off, my relationship with You is at a whole new level! Thank you, Jesus, I'm done!" But the Bible says that the righteousness of God is revealed from faith to faith.

Wow. I discovered that means that God still wants to take us higher and show us even more of what a deepened relationship with Him can reveal. No matter what stage of life or business you're currently in, God still has more for us to do. There is a new level, a new dimension of faith that we have yet to experience. So, what is your **Go Beyond** that God has given you today? What is it that God wants to do in your life that you need to trust Him fully for that you know you can't do in your own strength? Here are some things you can say when you talk to Him; "Lord, I have these plans for my family. I have these plans for my business. I have these plans in mind for myself, but today God, I give my plan back to you. Search me Lord. Search my heart and my mind. Have I…

- Made my plans big enough?
- Gone beyond my comprehension to totally rely on you?
- Considered you Lord and all of Your power, and the power that works in me?
- Considered all the things that You can do, all of your strength, all the connections that you can make?
- Really given it to you to go beyond what I have now?

Lord, this is what I've come up with in my brain and I believe I'm on the right track, but God in the areas where I haven't consulted You, I give it back to You as a blank canvas to do what You wish. Where You lead me from this point on, I will follow and I'm open to hearing what You have to say." Then stop and listen, being open to His response and ready to move where He leads.

Prayer

Father, I thank you Lord. I thank you God for every person who is reading this book. I thank you for every new business and every person who's thinking of starting a business. Lord, I thank you for dropping creative ideas and mind blowing perspectives into their spirit, and I just ask Lord that You give them boldness to just take that first step, that first leap of faith or that next leap of faith God in the name of Jesus, fully trusting that You are with them along the way.

Lord, I ask that You would just take them beyond their imagination. God, I just ask that you would take them beyond their thought processes and what their minds can comprehend. Our minds are nothing compared to what You can do. Lord, I ask that you would just show them what you have for them to do. God, show them the vision that you have for their lives and for their businesses. Let their desire to help your people or to meet a need be greater than any fear that tries to overtake them, because we know it's not about us at all, but it's all about You. Even when they might get discouraged or it seems like things are not working out in their favor, Your word encourages us to look to the hills whence cometh our help, because our help comes from You. If we stay focused on You, You will provide what we need. Show them the way God and hold their hand as they take each step forward with You.

Grant each person the boldness they need to keep moving forward in the name of Jesus. Lord God, I pray now for those who have existing businesses, even if everything is going well. Take them to the next level, God, not just for personal gain but also for the people or needs that you want them to serve. Reveal to them additional problems that need to be solved that can be additional streams of income and a legacy for them and their families. Let them not get complacent with their present level of faith, but help them to **Go Beyond** to a new level of faith, totally relying on You. You have placed in us everything that we need. I ask Lord that you would increase their faith right now in the name of Jesus. God, I ask that you would deepen their relationship with You and You would draw them closer. Take them higher in You. Sharpen their discernment and also help them to hear You clearly in the name of Jesus. From this day forth, it will no longer be business as usual. God, I ask that you would just reveal and bring them back to Your purpose, God, not ours because Your purpose is all that matters. You have the big picture, and even though we often think we want to know everything, we would most likely be so overwhelmed if we knew in the beginning where You wanted us to end up and all that's required to get there. So, we just ask that You continue to order our steps, God, in Your will and Your way.

I thank you Lord for bringing them before great men and helping them to move when You've orchestrated those divine connections. I ask Lord that you would even quiet that small voice that often comes after You've told us to do something that requires our faith to ignite. You tell us to do something and then in an instant, here comes that voice of the enemy that says we're not qualified or says that we're not on that level, or that voice that repeats the possibility. The enemy comes in that little voice that says we're not on that level, that voice that repeats the possibility that if we ask the answer will surely be no. That voice that says don't do it. Don't open your mouth. That small voice that says that your past isn't squeaky clean enough. That voice that says your credentials don't qualify you to be in the room. But little do we realize God that You want to use everything we have for Your glory, and we're already equipped with everything we need. Each of us is divinely qualified! Help us God to keep pushing to go beyond that little voice of fear and doubt, because the enemy has no power to defeat us. When we start to think about what we've been, or past failures, disappointments, or even mistakes, remind us God of Philippians 3:13-14 that says, "Forgetting the things that are behind and reaching forth to the things that are before. I press on toward the mark, (toward the goal), for the prize of the high calling of God in Christ Jesus."

It's so wonderful to know that once we've repented and asked You for forgiveness for whatever is in our past, we can forget the things that are behind us knowing You have washed us whiter than snow. What an amazing love You have for us God. And the even better news is that once we've overcome, You can use those things as a testimony to not only help our healing process but to help somebody else. So, we rebuke that small voice right now in the mighty, matchless name of Jesus, and thank you for giving us boldness above and beyond our own strength. God so often we get frustrated. God, we sometimes feel defeated, but during those times we're so often trying to do things in our own strength. Help us to clearly define Your plan for us that You created when You formed us in our mother's womb. Jeremiah 29: 11 says, "For I know the plans I have for you, plans to prosper you and not to harm you. Plans to give you a hope and a future." Another translation says, "plans to give you an expected end."

We are children of the King. God remind us of who we are in You. There is no limit on what You can do. Hallelujah. We thank you Lord for giving us this subject today of ***Going Beyond***, and we love You so much for caring enough to keep us encouraged to believe You for more, In Jesus' name. Amen and Amen.

I'll leave you with something I found interesting. When God gave me the subject, **Go Beyond**, I kept thinking, "I've heard that phrase somewhere before," but couldn't place it. When I finally looked it up, it's actually also the slogan of a former marketing campaign from Toyota, but theirs was, "Let's Go Beyond." So, I decided to look it up on online and I found this quote they used in an advertisement. It says,

Beyond Inspiration

"Let's go beyond everything we know. Let's embrace everything we don't. Let's not just look toward the future, but define it. We've learned that inspiration doesn't favor those who sit still. So, let's be bold, ambitious, even unconventional, because that's where big ideas come from. Ideas that not only take you places you can find on a map, but also ones that you can find in your heart. Let's go places together."

Wow, don't you love that? It's so amazing how this can be applied to what God is saying to us today. From this day on, let's continue to challenge each other to not just do what's comfortable or status quo, but to be open to **Going Beyond** in Jesus' name. I can't wait to see what He has in store as we let go and let God. Ready? Let's Go!

Questions for Reflection:

- In what area of my life have I been doing things my way and not consulting God or considering He has the ultimate plan?
- How can I take my faith in God to a new level by completely trusting Him?
- In what ways can I increase my time with God to strengthen my relationship with Him? How can I better create an environment where I can talk to and hear Him more clearly?

Bio

Kelli K. Fisher is a Certified Life and Relationship Coach, Certified Matchmaker, keynote speaker, and co-author of the critically acclaimed book, "Relationship DUOvers." Affectionately known throughout the industry and the world as ½ of "The Matchmaking DUO," Kelli's goal is to help women (and men) of power balance their career, personal, and love life by teaching how to effectively blend all three. As a divorced mother of 3 daughters, she took the faith leap with her young girls in tow to transition from corporate America to become a successful entrepreneur. Kelli often shares how her faith and trust in God for each step of her life's journey, which has been filled with many ups and downs, has activated a mindset of believing God for more even when it seems impossible. Connect with Kelli by following her @KellikFisher on all social media. **Learn more at thematchmakingduo.com or kellikfisher.com (coming soon).**

From Good to Fertile Ground

Kelly Janine Joyner

I want to start with a scripture we all know and love. We have quoted it many times and used it in sermons and as a reference point of encouragement.

Galatians 6:9 (KJV) states:

> *"And let us not be weary in well doing: for in due season we shall reap, if we faint not."*

I love this scripture! The bible talks frequently about sowing and reaping as well as harvesting after our due season! As a matter of fact, there are over 70+ bible verses that directly or indirectly refer to a harvest!

There is sowing time and there is reaping of that which was sown. Seed time and harvest time! The examples of sowing, reaping, and harvesting come from those that farm the land or till the ground. Everything we consume comes from the Earth. A seed is planted, cultivated, and it grows. Our hope is that what is planted will yield a necessary and good crop that can be harvested for use. What we see in the grocery store, neat and pretty, most likely began as a seed.

The typical or normal harvesting process begins with a planted seed. That seed receives the necessary nutrients from the ground, sun, and rain. All those things together allow the soil around the seed to provide the proper nutrients for growth. Proper growth. Abundant growth. However, there are times when the Earth is not ready or prepared to provide proper nutrients. They are just not there! The farmer has to then plant what is called a cover crop. Now, the cover crop is not necessarily for the seed, but the cover crop is for the ground! And, why is that? Often, what a farmer will use for cover crop is consumable by humans. Sometimes, they will use peanuts, certain greens like mustard or even kale. Mostly, however, what is planted for cover crop are plants that humans would never consume, like certain grasses - fescue, and rye grasses, etc.

The purpose of planting the cover crop is to ensure the ground, which is already good, can also be fertile! So that what is sown into this newly fertile ground will be provided all the nutrients and protection needed. Once that crop is ready to be harvested, it will have come from such a healthy place that it can only produce greatness!

So, how does all of this relate to entrepreneurship? Men and women of God who have businesses, have all had times in their lives where we felt like we had done so much, sown so much into our business and yet...nothing was being produced! We've planted, watered, and waited on an increase and still nothing! Nothing has yielded. There was no fruit, no harvest... nothing! We wrote the book that only our mothers purchased. We had conferences that only our best friends showed up to. What was happening?

God was preparing us for greater! We were always "good" ground, but God needed to "cover" us in order to make us fertile ground! Producing ground! So, during that covering when it appeared nothing was happening, we continued to write! We continued to preach and teach! We continued to pour into others! We continued to read and study! We continued to hone the gift that God had given us! Not for our perfection, but for His Glory! That book you wrote sis, it needed a workbook or God downloaded something so powerful, you needed a 2nd edition!

God needed to remind you that in spite of what your parents said, regardless of what your ex said, no matter what others have whispered behind your back...YOU ARE GOOD GROUND! Now, you are also fertile ground! Often, God needs to cover you for a season so that what

He is producing in you will be used for the His people and for His Glory!! What you produced last year wasn't ready for God's people. It wasn't ready for the marketplace. It wasn't edible! But God! What He has prepared you for, in this season, is not only edible, but it is something people can FEAST on!

You are great simply because of who our Daddy is! Greatness is in your DNA! It is your birthright! It is who you were created to be! It may have taken a minute, but you are on the right track! You haven't given up and neither has God! Don't worry about what didn't work last year, it will be bigger and better this next harvest! Your faith commands it!

Prayer:

Dear Heavenly Father, we thank you for loving us! We thank you God for establishing us in your Kingdom! We thank you for preparing us, for covering us all these years only for the harvest that is to come! We thank you that we are walking into our *due season*! Right now! We haven't given up, we haven't thrown in the towel, we haven't walked away, but we have been faithful, and we have persevered! We kept growing by *Your* Grace! We were steadfast over the years and even though we often thought of giving up, it was your promises we remembered! It was *Your* faithfulness we stood on! It was *Your* word we continued to speak over our lives, our families, and our businesses. We have sown in tears, we have sown our finances, we have sown spiritually, and it was all for your Glory! So, God we are expecting that our harvest manifest now, in this season!

It is the year of emergence! We are coming out of all that we have been through! We've been through hell *and* high water, muck and mire, but we declare we are coming out! We are the crop you planted, and we are coming out of despair, depression, and discouragement! We are coming out of hurt, pain, and disappointments! This is our time to shine! This is our time to grow to even greater heights in you God!

Kelly Janine Joyner

You said in your word that eyes haven't seen; ears haven't heard, nor has it entered into the heart of man what you have prepared for us that love you! We are going beyond what we have even imagined! Glory to God!

We survived all the hell we went through in the past. But God we thank you right now! We did more than survive...we conquered it all! Yes God! We conquered not only for ourselves God, but we did it for others, too! We did it so they would see you God! See you in all your Glory! We did it so they would believe and benefit from the harvest! We stayed in the fight so they would benefit from the overflow and abundance you promised!

God, we believe favor is about to hit us in a mighty way! All of us who belong to you God! All of us who trust you...even when we do not understand, God we trust you and anticipate favor in our lives from this day forward!

God, connect us supernaturally! Sever those relationships that will not produce your harvest in our lives. Sever those relationships that are stifling and hindering to us, God. Connect us God to those we are supposed to be connected to in this season and time. We wait and expect divine appointments from now on! We no longer beg anyone to be on our team, no longer beg for anyone to help or support because God you have already established our connections! You have already divinely appointed our teams, and God we thank you!

We stand in agreement that this is not a season God, for seasons come and seasons go, but God this is a *life shift*! It is not seasonal! It is not predicated upon others, but only because of you God! This shift is a never-ending shift and has been established in the earth because you first established it in your Kingdom! And God we will walk into this new life shift victoriously! We will walk into this new life shift expectantly! We thank you God that every new idea, every invention, every new business idea be downloaded immediately and sealed with the blood of your precious son, Jesus! This is a very pivotal moment in

Beyond Inspiration

our lives God! Minds are changing, hearts are healing, and businesses are growing and turning around!

More importantly God, this is a pivotal moment in our faith and our relationship with you! We thank you God that it is already done. What you have established here in the Earth is already done! We are no longer asking you to fix it Jesus...you already did! We no longer ask you for a breakthrough, we already broke through last night at midnight and we are already victorious! We have turned the corner and completely surrender to you and your will! Our faith has increased as you continue to cover us and make us strong!

You did it God! We thank you God for setting us up to succeed! Even in those times when we thought we were failing. Those times when you were covering us, and we felt alone and confused. When the enemy tried to tell us that nobody was listening, that nobody would come, that we misheard you on our purpose. When he tried to plant seeds of doubt, you planted even greater seeds of purpose! Even in those times, God we thank you for setting us all up to succeed!

We realize now that you were calling us to a greater, higher promise! You were simply establishing who we are. You were creating and building our confidence in you, and in who you created us to be! You were pushing us out into the forefront, not for our own glory, but all for the Glory of God! We thought we were looking foolish and uncertain, but someone was watching and learning from us! Someone who wrote a book years ago, is now being asked to turn that book into a stage play, or turn that book into workbooks and a series, and finally a course at a University! Someone who had only 10-15 people in attendance at their last conference is now prepared for the 1000's that will be at their next one!

God, we thank you that anytime we did fail, we learned! We learned that you were preparing us for our future successes! We thank you and commit to you God, that we will be good stewards over all you bless us with from this day forward. We will not squander our blessings. We will not take for granted our blessings. The favor that hits our lives will hit us like never before! All because we were faithful during our covering season! We continued to plant, we continued to sow, and we will continue to reap all that we have prayed for, cried over, and what we have dutifully sown! We were already good ground, but now God you have made us fertile! Everything that is harvested from this day forward will be for our good, but mostly for your Glory! Thank you, God!

There were times when it seemed as if every time we said yes to you God, the enemy tried to stop us! The enemy tried to bring us trouble! Something else happened and things began to fall apart! But God, we thank you that even your *no* is greater than man's yes! We thank you that if *You* say yes, it matters not what man says! So, we keep pressing, we keep moving forward in you God! Our faithfulness will be rewarded and honored by you God!

God, you also honor our obedience. You honor those times when we wanted to give up and give in! We wanted to tap out, but you wouldn't let us, and we thank you! No matter what God, we hung in there because of our faith, and we are grateful you hung in there with us! We have learned that understanding you and your ways is never a requirement for trusting you and your ways! When others told us to quit, we stayed the course! When others told us we weren't any good, we stayed the course! When they told us to "just go get a job," we stayed the course! And you kept whispering that we were on the right path! Thank you, God!

God from this day forward, we will rise in our authority! We will rise in the authority you have given us! We will rise up in our Kingdom Authority and be all you called us to be! Not what others have said, but what you have said! We will do all you have called us to do, not what others think we should do. We no longer will conform to the world's order, but we yield to your will only! Glory to God!

Anyone who does not have Kingdom Authority to speak into our lives, remove them from our lives immediately! So, we march into this time

God, not worried about what anyone else has said, not worried about what happened before, not even thinking about the past, but embracing our future! We have full assurance that our steps have been ordered by you God! We will not live in regret nor do we think we've wasted time, but we trust your Holy Word and your promises for our future.

God, we thank you that we don't walk in error, but we walk in Divine wisdom and authority! We thank you for that wisdom and authority! God, send your ministering angels to protect and guide us to those who will speak holiness and righteousness into our lives. Continue to order our footsteps and navigate our paths. God, continue to move obstacles out of our way and stop us from taking the old ways of yesterday into tomorrow! We value our favor with you Oh God! We will continue to honor you with all you have entrusted to us! Reveal to us who is to go with us and whose time has come to an end! Thank you, Jesus! Let them drop off in Jesus name! Let the relationships be cut off without hurt or hard feelings but give them the understanding that they were not needed to fulfill the assignment on our lives! They were not needed to take us to our next levels in you, Oh God! They were not sent by your divine appointment! We thank you God!

We have been to the prison, and we have been in the pit, but God this is our year of the palace! This is our year of promotion! Hallelujah! Our favor with you extends to favor with man! Let them see you God in us! Let them know without doubt that it was you that sent us! God, we believe what you told us and what you have shown us, and we fight to honor that vision!

We will finish this race God! We will finish it faithfully and with your guidance! We, as entrepreneurs, every day are taking our rightful place in the marketplace and you are pleased! We are introducing you to those who would have never stepped into a church or bible study. We are opening minds and changing lives! We thank you for the opportunity to serve you in this way God! We will be bold in our desire to serve you in this way! We will be bold about who we are and whose we are! We will be bold about our calling and our purpose! We will be bold in our assignments as well! We no longer question you or what you told us. As your children, we know your voice and another we will not follow! We thank you that the mountains we face Father, we boldly take them on, knowing they shall be moved! It shall be moved, and it shall be conquered!

We don't have to worry about it God, because you have already called us victorious! Your will for our lives has already been established! God if we made $100,000 last year, this is our year of double fold increase! If we sold to 15 to 20 to even 100 people last year, that number will be doubled, tripled, and even quadrupled this year! God, we thank you for increase! Supernatural increase! The power is shifting God! We can feel the shift! The shift is not only in our businesses, but in our ministries as well! The shift is in our families and in our homes! We know it! The world knows it! We are pouring into your people as you pour into us and God, we thank you!

God, we seek your face in everything we do! Matthew 6:33 is our mandate and our cry! We no longer seek your hand, but we seek your presence and your face! Glory to God!

So now God, we have our marching orders and as we move forward in faith, we thank you! We thank you God for the opportunity to continue to plant, sow, and harvest! We thank you God, that even though storms come to break us, you allow us to grow stronger because of them! We may bend in the storms, but we will not break! We thank you for our continued growth! Every year we grow closer to you, and every year we grow deeper in your word! Thank you, God! Amen!

Questions for Reflection:

- After reading this chapter how has your view regarding your seed time and harvest changed?
- How will you respond going forward during the "cover crop" seasons of your life?
- Reflect on a time in your life where you now understand God was covering you and preparing you for a greater harvest.

Bio

Kelly is a native of the Northern Virginia area and now calls Charlotte, NC her home. She is known for her many gifts, such as being a two-time best-selling author, public speaker, and a Hope Cultivator Life Coach. Those that know her describe her as a fun-loving, encouraging, and a believer of doing all things with a spirit of excellence. She is a go-getter, trailblazer, and inspires many to live life to the fullest. She is currently penning her *third* book, chronicling her journey of infertility and hopelessness to a redefined hope in God's plan for her life! Kelly is also an amazing motivational speaker whose main goal is to not only motivate those around her, but to also empower them to improve their lives by rebuilding their dreams. She has worked with everyone from CEO'S, teachers and preachers, to working Moms and college students. She helps women become all they were meant to be in the home, school, and workplace, as well as the entrepreneurial marketplace. She refuses to allow those who work with her to quit or give up on their dreams! Her motto is simple - With God all things are possible, so let's do the work! **Learn more about Kelly at kellyjoyner.fathomrealty.com**

Dare to Believe...

You Are
Leading the Way and
Changing the Game!

Leading While Bleeding

Youlisha Bundy

There is a certain question that comes to my heart, and at times I feel some kind of way about it based on my own life circumstances. That question is, *"Should you be leading while bleeding?"* Should you be leading while you're going through great tests, trials, and tribulations? Should you be leading when you are suffering from a broken heart such as a loss of a loved one, a divorce, relationship issue, or a child acting up? I want you to think about the question. As you are being positioned by your pain, your trials are the things that you have been through and overcome. While you are being conditioned on the inside in your relationship with God, you will have to consider whether you should be leading while you are going through.

As a coach, we don't just tell you what to do. In fact, we ask you the important questions that will make you come up with your own action plan of what you plan to do to implement what it is that you need to implement. So, should you be leading while bleeding? What happens when

- Business is booming and going great?
- You've got your calendar filled with clients and engagements?
- Profit is coming in and things are flowing, you're prospering, and your ministry is growing?
- Your writing is flowing?

What happens when all is going well, but life happens, and God allows something that literally crushes your spirit and breaks your heart. It comes in and knocks you off your feet. What do you do when this happens right after you have been booked or have a commitment you've made? When that happens, right at that moment, what can you do?

My answer, as I thought about this often, is yes at times and at times, I'd say no. I'll tell you why. God told me to share this testimony with you. The purpose of this testimony is not to put fear in anyone. There's no fear, the word of God told us to expect trials and tribulation. I really believe that those reading this will see great strides in their businesses, their ministries, their coaching practices, and in their lives. I believe that we will experience great success and prosper like never before.

In 2017, I had the opportunity to travel and minister in song and worship at an intimate women's conference. I live in Virginia and had the opportunity to go and minister near Augusta, Georgia, an area I had never been to. At the time I was actually pregnant. Those that have heard my testimony are my followers on social media, my clients, and my friends and family. They all know my husband and I have had an interesting journey while trying to grow our family. Leading up to it, I was so excited. I was approaching this pregnancy by faith; I was believing God. I was speaking His promises and life over myself, over my pregnancy, and I was determined at this time to do what God would have me to do… no matter what.

My husband, who is so supportive, took off from work and business to drive me down to Georgia. He told me he'd be my, what some people might call, armor bearer. Basically, he'd be there for me to do everything he could to make sure I had everything I needed, ensure everything went smooth, and that I was ready for this particular event. As we began to drive down, I noticed that I was having more uncomfortable cramps. They were bad enough that I was taking Tylenol, and I usually don't take anything. They were definitely feeling a little more intense than normal. Unfortunately, we had had previous miscarriages in the past, and to be honest, the cramps were getting a little bit more than maybe your normal pregnancy cramps. But I just began to speak the word of God over myself. And, like I told you, I was committed to go and do what God would have me to do. I was so excited about Him expanding my territory. So, I headed to Georgia to minister in song and in worship, which is one of the things I love to do. I think I mentioned it to my husband. We prayed, and we kept it moving. We got to Georgia, checked in our hotel, had dinner, and rested. As I prepared for the conference the next day, I remember feeling a little uncomfortable but probably didn't sleep the best, which happens a lot of times before I have to minister. I don't sleep the best the night before. I didn't think much of it, but I got up that morning and let's just say I saw signs that seemed to confirm the pregnancy might be ending as another miscarriage. Here I am getting up, literally getting dressed, trying to get pretty and get ready to go minister at this women's conference and I am having a miscarriage.

I continued without asking myself that question, should I be leading while I'm bleeding? I literally was making that decision at that time. I just began to think and pray: "Lord, you know you're allowing me to go through whatever you're allowing me to go through. And I've got to depend and trust in you." I came all this way. There was no way I was not going to go through with what He called me to do, which on this day was leading others in worship. I figured, "Hey, I'm just going to worship from a true and honest place." Honestly, at that moment I literally just began to worship. I told my husband what was going on and he prayed with me. I went in that bathroom and as I got ready, I was worshipping. We know when we worship, when we praise God, when we speak to Him that His presence comes and inhabits us wherever we are. I felt His presence! I felt His strength! I felt His prompting to, "Yes, go forward", that He would be with me, that He would be my strength. So… that is exactly what I did.

I went forward and I ministered in worship. Honestly, I don't remember the exact songs I sang. I only remember one of them, which was Clean by Natalie Grant, but I know that it was from just a pure place. I'm sure there were some moments of, "God you're my everything, God you are my healer", but I just worshipped from where I was at the time of needing, depending, and trusting in God alone. God showed up in a beautiful way in that place. Not only did He show up in the worship, but He showed up for me with the speakers, and in those that were speaking into my life. I literally had people come and give me a word from God, and I didn't tell anyone anything about what was going on in my life at that moment. But let me tell you, it was a God moment for me. You know when you have those moments where you know God is real and that He's for us. I'm telling you, at the moment, when you are at your weakest… that is when His strength is made perfect in you.

So, should you be leading while bleeding? I used to have an issue with it. It's probably because I'm literal and a TMI type person, but I would think no because you are going to bleed on someone else. When you make a choice to lead while you bleed, you have to consider if someone else might have to experience your pain. Someone else might have to experience you being out of character. To be honest with you, my husband and I have been through some difficult things trying to conceive. Years back, I called myself leading while bleeding and I wasn't taking care of myself. I wasn't doing what I needed to in order to heal or at least put a patch on my mess, my hurt, or my pain. My emotions were all over the place. I'm sure there were some people that I may have damaged my testimony with because I didn't take a moment to seek the Healer. I didn't take a moment to pause for myself to make sure I was depending on God to be my strength and not just trying to go forward in my own strength to meet commitments.

When you're asking yourself about leading while bleeding, seek God's reply. I did this by inquiring of Him, "Lord, do we have to lead while we bleed?" I'm going to be honest, what I heard Jesus say was, No! And you know why He said no? He said you don't have to lead while you're bleeding because I led while I was bleeding. When Jesus went to the cross, He was leading while bleeding and He did it so we don't have to.

Am I saying that you're not going to have to lead or show up in pain? No, I'm not saying that. Am I saying that you're not going to have to show up and still do what you're called to do? You're going to have to still go to the business meeting, still preach, still teach, and still pray for others. But you don't have to go out there with open wounds that you have not allowed God's love to cover for you. You're not out there by yourself. You're not out there alone, but you can allow God to come in and at least put that band aid of healing on it for a moment, so that you can do what He's called for you to do without bleeding and spilling anything that is ungodly. While we are still called to go, we have to allow Him to deal with anything that would tarnish His image on us or on anyone else. I've been through so much in my journey of leading and still having to show up. He's never allowed me to show up in the workplace and just be a team member, but always somehow being called out to be a leader. I've had to show up at my worship center. I've always been called out to be a leader when at the time it felt like my life, at least in some areas, felt like it was in shambles. Yet, it felt like God was calling me to show up.

I'm realizing that in the seasons of pressing and enduring, He is working out something awesome in us, and He is positioning us in the right place to do what He's called us do. He is building our testimony and more. But what do you do? The Lord deals with me a lot on how to do things practically, with simple steps, to be able to implement what He's asking us to do. When things come up, we're prepared and have some actions that we can do. What do you do when you know you have those important business meetings? I know that there are some of those who were writing their chapters of this book and I promise you, some of them had to fight trials and tribulations and battles during the process. Some of them had to overcome things and they still showed up and met all the tasks and deadlines required. You must know what you can do so that you can still show up and not bleed mess on the people. Here are some practical things that God gave me to share with you. They are tips to help you continue when you have those things you simply have to do even though life has come in and maybe crushed you in that moment. Life has come in and there's some area in which, if you can be honest, you're weak. There's some area that's not looking right and making you feel like you're disqualified, but it's actually qualifying you.

Here are some things you could do

Believe it or not, even ministering and teaching this is something I wasn't doing, and it almost messed up my testimony. It actually may have with some, but God's grace is sufficient, and I thank Him for covering my multitude of sins. He does know our hearts and He judges them accordingly. He knows what our motives are, but the first thing that we need to do is ***get close to God.*** When you are going through you better run to Him. You've got to get close to Him like never before. And I know that, we all say, we run to God when we're in trouble. And then when things are all good, we don't pray as hard. We don't pray as often. We don't spend as much time with Him. But I'm here to tell you God loves you. Even if that was the case for you, when you're going through, by all means run close to God. His arms are open and ready to receive you. People are in different places in their faith. So, sometimes they hear someone say get close to God, and they will say well, what does that mean? Well, one thing you can do is encourage yourself in the Lord. You remind yourself of God's promises and His promises are in His word. Most importantly, when you are going through something that is messing with your heart, something that is hurting you in your very core, that makes your soul hurt or cry… When you are experiencing the pain that makes you moan, where you don't even have words to pray… never forget how much God loves you. Never forget the love of God.

In those dark and painful times, Satan will try to come in and give you thoughts and say, "God is allowing you to go through this. You know He is not really for you. You're going through this because you did that." He comes with thoughts of condemnation and he really wants to take your focus off of God's love for you. Do not listen to him. Instead, remind yourself of God's promises. Remind yourself that He loves you. Remind yourself that He said He will never leave you nor forsake you. Take every negative thought captive as quickly as possible and replace it with what the word of God says. In 2 Corinthians 12:9-10, we look at Paul. Paul is a good example of someone that was leading and doing what he was called to do, but also faced much persecution, and had many issues and different things happen to him. Scripture tells us that he was literally being tormented. Often times, people that have a high spiritual call on their lives get tormented. God may allow some things to happen. He may allow you to have to overcome some things. Why? Because He has to prepare you for the position that He has created for you. Paul said he sought the Lord to please remove this thorn, to remove this torment from him. And God said, my grace is all you need. My power works best in your weakness. This changed Paul's perspective. His confession became, *I'm glad to boast about my weaknesses, so the power of Christ can work through me.*

There was a time I wouldn't have shared my testimony or the things that I have been through that are real and painful, but I can boast about it because in my weaknesses, the power of Christ works through me. I promise you, some of you reading this, if you think back, there are some moments that you wonder,

- How did you get through that meeting without crying?
- How did you get through that speaking engagement?
- How were you able to sing that worship song knowing you didn't know where your children were?
- How did you get through that?

Well, God's strength came in when you were weak. This is why it is imperative to make sure you get closer to God.

The second thing you have to do is **inquire of the Lord what you should do.** There's no cookie cutter answer. Should you be leading while bleeding? Should you still show up? How do you know when you need to sit this one out? It depends how big the issue is, or how much it's impacting you, and whether or not this is a time for you to press. This could be something for you to endure as a good soldier. How do you know? You must inquire of the Lord. You have to ask Him what you should do, and what is this? This just happened, do I need to step back? Do I need to spend more time with my family? Do I need to maybe put something on hold? When you inquire of the Lord, these are some options He may give you. I think everyone should take a little mini break. You have to take a break, and that break might be minutes, hours, or even days.

I remember when I was going to that conference, my husband came with me to help me. I actually told him that I wanted to drive myself from the hotel to the place the conference was being held. He was concerned and he kept asking me, "Are you sure? Are you sure?" And I said, "Yes, I want to drive myself." Why? Because I needed a break. I needed a few minutes. And again, I was in a hotel room. I wasn't home, and I needed a few minutes where I could be one on one with God. I knew that I needed to literally cry out to Him, if I can be honest with you. I wanted to drive myself, and I did just that. I cried out to the Lord.

I was completely honest with Him. I wept some, I did what I had to do. So, for me, I had to take a break and this time I had a few minutes to myself. Maybe you need to take a few minutes and steal away to let it all out, you know, cry it out. Maybe you won't be with someone like I was. I was with my husband, who covered me in prayer at that moment. Maybe you need to reach out to a sister or brother to pray for you. Your minute may look different from mine, but you need to take one if you can. Truth be told, we all can find some minutes or hours. Depending on what you're going through, if you experienced great loss by losing a loved one, you might need days.

Sometimes you need to take a break and allow your soul to heal. Again, leading while bleeding, leading while going through, leading while in pain, going through tests and trials, that's one thing. But bleeding out because you're acting on your emotions; acting out of character and doing those things can really mess up your testimony. So, if you need a break, take a break.

The third thing He may tell you to do is **delegate**. He may give you someone that may come up in your spirit. Maybe you were supposed to do a tele class, but there are some powerful people you are connected with. There have been times that I have delegated. I've had a scheduled call and I was able to delegate and ask someone else to come and teach my flock at that particular time. Honestly, they didn't even know why I asked them to do that, but I was going through a healing process. If God brings someone in your spirit, a good leader knows how to delegate. You've got to delegate to someone else. Maybe you are in a traditional business environment, then you might need to delegate some of your menial tasks so that you can have more time to work on your healing. You may have to postpone or reschedule something, and there is nothing wrong with that. Leaders have to do that. They have to change their schedules. I know your schedule may be in ink, but they can be changed. Most of them are electronic schedules and things are meant to change. If you have to postpone something so that you can truly show up the way God would have you to show up, postpone and reschedule. Inquire of the Lord if that's something that you need to do.

Know when you need to get help and get it! Know when you need help other than just your sisters or brothers in Christ. Know when you need to now go and see a counselor, or when you need to go see the Matters of the Heart Coach! Know when you need to maybe go and sit and talk to the leaders of your church. Know when you need to seek help! There comes a time when we all have to seek out some type of help. We need someone that has been there and done that. We need someone that can, you know, share their testimony with us. Some practical things to help us in healing. For example: if all hell is breaking loose in your home, maybe you need to take a break and call in a family counselor. Know when you need help and get it!

Lastly and most importantly, a few years ago God told me to **keep my focus on my why**. It has helped me like never before. I remember my why, and when I think of it, I think of other men and women that have been through some of the things that I've been through. If I allow the issues of life or the matters of the heart to make me completely shut down, then what God called me to put out into the world and impact His kingdom will not get done. Therefore, I remember my why. Jesus gave us the example in Hebrews 12:1-2 (NLT). It says,

> *"Therefore, since we are surrounded by such a huge crowd of witnesses to the life of faith, let us strip off every weight that slows us down, especially the sin that so easily trips us up. And let us run with endurance the race God has set before us."*

He says we do this by keeping our eyes on Jesus, the champion who initiates and perfects our faith, because of the joy awaiting Him. He endured the cross disregarding His shame, and now He is seated in the place of honor beside God's throne, and Jesus is our example. So, when you are going through those hard times and pain, trials, and tribulations are coming into your life to position you, keep your eyes on Jesus and remember the joy set before you. Remember the flock that God has given you. Remember the people who God has called you to impact. Remember the kingdom and your part in the Kingdom. Remember what you're supposed to build and what you're supposed to put in place, and let that be the joy set before you. Keep your eyes on that and disregard the shame. All of us are going through something.

I promise you the people you look up to, go to for encouragement and guidance, hear are in your area for an event and you drop everything to attend; there are times before they get on that stage when their hearts are broken. There are things going on in their households that we know nothing about, but what makes them different is that they did not forget their why. What makes them different is that they have learned to get closer to Jesus in those moments, and all you are seeing is the treasure that is in them. When you are at your weakest, God can come in and completely have His way and be the strength for you.

Prayer:

Lord, I thank you for this opportunity and I thank you for every heart that is reading this right now. I pray for those that are broken. Lord, your word tells us that you are close and near to the brokenhearted. God, I feel your presence even right now. I know that you are near and that your love is covering and literally holding some people as they are reading this prayer, even as a blanket Lord God. Lord, there may be those whose marriages are not where it should be and it's pulling on their heart. Yet, in the meantime, they're experiencing great things in business and ministry. But when they come home things aren't right. Maybe they don't know where their children are, or they're being disobedient, or they're not acting right, or maybe something's going on in their health and in their body, and they feel like it will disqualify them. But I thank you that on today God, you are reminding people that it is all working together for our good, for your purpose and for your glory God. I pray Lord God for those who may have already encountered setbacks in business and ministry, for those who are beginning to get their calendars booked up, and there's things that they have to show up for even with issues happening. Lord, I pray that they won't count it as a surprise. That instead they will do what your word says and count it all joy. That they would count it all joy when they experience tests and trials. I pray that you will help us to remember the joy of our salvation. I pray, Lord God, that you will help us to remember the joy of seeing the souls that get saved when we are obedient. The joy of seeing the lives that are changed when we are obedient in putting out into the world and into the marketplace what you have put in us.

Thank you, Lord God, for those who have a marketplace ministry, but may not yet realize they have a ministry. Lord, but when they show up, when they go to the meeting, Lord, there's no fighting, Lord God, but there's peace and there's decisions that get made, because when they come in, they change the atmosphere. I pray that you will help them to know, Lord God, that when we endure different situations and we overcome, that's when our relationship with you gets stronger because we had to trust you, because we had to test our faith, because we showed up asking you to show up and speak through us. When we showed up and we still ministered, and we still taught, and we still had the meeting, and we still did the business in spite of what we were going through, we saw you have your way. It strengthens our relationship with you just like in the natural Lord that when someone proves their love to us, Lord God, not just by words or by their mouth, Lord God, but we literally see their love because they take care of us. We see their love because they show up, support us, and do the things that we need them to do.

God, when we are at our weakest point, that's when we really see you show up. You show up for us every day and every moment. You're with us, Lord God, you're strengthening us. You're anointing us. You're filling, you're preparing us God every moment of every day. When we're on the mountain top, when we're achieving, you're the one filling us up. You're the one working through us. But when we are weak, my God, when our heart is broken., when we still show up in obedience to you God because we inquired and you told us to still go. We inquired and you told us to still speak. We inquired and you told us to still show up. When we do that at our weakest and your anointing takes over and has its way. God our relationship with you grows in ways that we can't even imagine.

We never can doubt you when we have seen you work when we've been at our lowest. I pray this year we will see you work like never before and I thank you God that you are positioning us. I thank you that for the things that hurt us on the inside God, that you are the God that also heals the things that we can't touch, that heals the things that we can't name, the things that we can't take a pill for, the things that we can't go see the regular doctor for. I thank you God that your healing power heals those things as well. Heal broken hearts even now, Lord God! Shower your love Lord, even now. Encourage hearts, fix families, fix relationships God, even now, regulate minds and bring peace to the people that are troubled in their spirits. In the name of Jesus, we pray. Amen.

Questions for Reflection:

- Are you currently leading while bleeding? If so, in what area or areas?
- What are some of the tasks you have for business and/or ministry that you can delegate?
- Have you identified available resources to help you to successfully continue in business and/or ministry? Ex. Counselor, Coach, Assistant etc.

Bio

Youlisha Bundy is the Matters of the Heart Coach. Her vision is to help those who are dealing with the matters of the heart such as abuse, grief, divorce, rejection, and infertility to find healing so they can continue to pursue their God given purpose. She is a proud wife, mother, professional, and business owner. She is a licensed Convergence Spiritual Cleansing Specialist and Convergence Coach through the Convergence Center, LLC. Since 2013, she has been working with clients individually, in small groups, and larger events to help them find healing for their most intimate matters of the heart. She regularly shares inspiration and practical steps to help people overcome issues via her blog found at www.themattersoftheheart.com, books, teleconferences, social media, and client sessions.

Youlisha loves to laugh and has a way of breaking complex issues down in a way that makes them understandable, relatable, and that helps you do the work!

The Game Changing Shot

Cheryl C. Riley

As the mom of three athletes, I have spent countless hours in the bleachers of a stadium, court, or some other sporting facility. I have been the quintessential spectator mom and at times a loudly cheering educator. Whether it was for my personal children or my school surrogates, it has been my joy to support them all in their athletic endeavors. Sports can serve as excellent object lessons. Since young people understand games, I often use them when speaking with my students and even adults. I know the example below will be one to which you can also relate.

In the mid 1960's, there rose a basketball phenom by the name of Lewis Alcindor. We would later come to know this young man as Kareem Abdul Jabbar, member of the NBA Hall of Fame. In high school, at 7'1, Lewis led Power Memorial Academy to the New York Catholic Championship, finishing the season with a 71-game winning streak. His talent would gain him entrance into the University of California at Los Angeles (UCLA). In those days, freshmen did not play on the varsity team. Not good for that number one nationally ranked varsity team, as they would be defeated by the freshman team led by Alcindor who would score 31 points and snag 21 rebounds. That win gave the freshman team bragging rights. He was definitely a force to be reckoned with. Alcindor's height was his super power, his edge and everyone knew it. In 1967, during his sophomore year, the NCAA would disallow dunking. This became known as the "Lew Alcindor Rule." The system would not allow Lew to be great, to employ his edge. For the next nine years no one was able to dunk in college basketball. Game changing!

Merriam Webster defines a game changer as an event or procedure that affects a significant shift in the current manner of doing or thinking about something. Lew had shifted the course of basketball. No longer able to use his power move, it was obvious the average player was no match for him given his height advantage, which increased his dunking ability. With this tool no longer available, what would he do now? How would he respond? The mission of the game had not changed; put the ball in the basket while preventing your opponent from doing the same, right? Alcindor had to have some adverse feelings about the matter. Though his name was not in the official ruling, everyone knew he was the catalyst for it. He had a decision to make. Do I quit? Should I complain about how unfair the ruling was? It wasn't his fault he was 7'1." Though they had taken away the dunk, they had not taken away his gift, his edge, or his super power. He still had his height. Now, how could he take his gift and still get the ball in the basket. Lew had already changed the game of basketball to the point that they changed the rules of the game, but now what? His response, he didn't quit. He didn't pout. He birthed a new shot called the Sky Hook.

The sky hook wasn't new, but he had the capability to make the shot from greater distances than anyone else. It would become his trademark shot. Kareem would later be crowned the highest scoring player of all time during his career, and he was well respected for his skillset. These had to be challenging times for Lew, but you never heard of him behaving negatively or speaking ill of the system. Job 9:27 tells us,

> *"Though I say I will forget my complaint I will leave off my sad countenance and be cheerful."*

Lew made the decision to make the best of his circumstance. To be the catalyst of change even when it appeared the system resisted him.

As we transition through life from one year to the next or birthday to the next, it is customary to evaluate what one has done with those days, then position one's self for the upcoming year. For Kareem, it was not the end of a year but the end of an era, yet the same process was taking place. What is it that you are reassessing and reflecting on? What adjustments must be made in order for you to operate in your gifting or super power? What is the thing that God has given you to move or to implement your game changing shot?

We all have our edge. We all have our 7'1" thing. The thing that sets us apart. Whether we are a thrifting maven possessing an eye for a bargain or a social media guru sharing our tricks of the trade, we must see beyond the gift to the calling. Is the thrifting about heaping items for my closet or a means of blessing others as we shop? Are we now positioning our families better financially so that we are able to give more to the Kingdom? We must recognize and realize that the gift, our anointing, is not just about us but about changing the game and the circumstances for those around us. It is purposed to bear witness of God's goodness toward His children.

We see this with Joseph in the book of Genesis. Joseph was the favored son of his father Jacob. The son of his beloved Rachel, Jacob unashamedly illustrated preferential treatment to Joseph supplying him with a beautiful coat of many colors. His brothers did not take kindly to this. To add salt to the wound Joseph would have a dream where the sun, moon, and 11 stars would bow down to him. He had two versions of the dream and shared them both with his family. They were livid. The dream spoke of things to come, but his brothers thought not so. They plotted to kill him, changed their minds, and sold him to the Midianites who sold him to Potiphar. And when he gets into the house of Potiphar, Potiphar recognizes that this man is in my house, and since he's been in my house, my house has been blessed. That's what happens with us when people encounter us and they recognize it. They realize when they have gotten into our presence and become connected with us, that they're going to be blessed. And as a result, Potiphar's house prospered. We know what ended up happening. Joseph ended up in prison because of a lie that Potiphar's wife told on him. Next, he goes to prison and prospers in the prison, and interprets the dream of the butler and the baker. He shares what is going to happen in his dream and it ends up happening. They're supposed to look out for him as a result of helping them out, but they didn't. Yet, even in that situation, he still ends up leading while in the prison. He's a game changer.

Joseph finally gets out when Pharaoh needs to have his dream interpreted. He is summoned to go before Pharaoh but he recognizes, "Before I go to Pharaoh, let me get myself together. Let me present myself properly." (Genesis 41:14) We too must do the same thing and pause long enough to get our game plan together. Whether its things in our physical appearance like getting our hair and nails done to preparing our content, we have to be ready before we go to present. So, he gets before Pharaoh. Pharaoh tells the dream, and Joseph interprets it. He has the strategy to solve the impending problem the dream reveals and shares his solution. A direct download from God that will change the lives of all Egypt, deliver the children of Israel, and have Joseph's family bowing down to him. Jeremiah 29:11 tells us,

> *"I know the plans that I have towards you, plans for good and not of evil to give you an expected end, a hope and a future."*

He had no idea that all the foolishness he had gone through with his brothers and in prison would bring him to this place. He had no idea it would lead him to the fulfillment of everyone else's dreams and needs for the family of Israel. So, he gets there and interprets Pharaoh's dream. After interpreting the dream, he now has to carry out the strategy.

God is using you to be the strategist and the survival plan. Joseph shares the plan and divvies out everybody's responsibilities. His family is now free from famine. They are now free from desolation because the dreamer, the strategist, the game changer, Joseph, was properly positioned to bring deliverance to the people. You too have the survival plan, not just for your individual business but for all of those you are connected with.

Kareem could not fully operate in what he was supposed to operate in because he was seven-foot-one and they attempted to place limits on him. The same way Joseph had been placed in the pit and in prison, Kareem was told not to dunk. Now he's in the position to where he is able to change the game for all of those around him. And in changing game he changes destinies. God is changing our destinies. God is changing the destinies of those that we encounter because of the gift that's on the inside of us. So just as Joseph did, just as an entire family, an entire lineage, legacies, not just for Israel, but for Egypt, even those who were not engrafted, who were not a part of Abraham, Isaac, and Jacob. Even those individuals got in on the plan. They were the ones who received the blessing because they were connected to those who were in the family of God. So those who are connected to you are going to be blessed. You are a game changer with a game changing shot. Iron, you are sharpened iron and not rusted metal. The hand of God is on your life in this year and beyond. Your legacies are being made as we speak. Lives are being changed. Things are being shifted because of the work you've put in and are about to do.

Kareem had prepared for years. He put in the work; he had gone to the gym. You have done the same thing by burning the midnight oil, the 2:00 a.m. hours, the books, the notes you've written, the game plans, the strategies you've devised. You have put in the work and now it's game time. Regardless of what the enemy or the system tries to put in your way, you are out of the pit! You are out of the prison! You are in victory, and you have the strategies! The strategies are now in operation and lives are being changed. It is about us being in a place of greatness, but it isn't just about us. We have not come to this place with God simply for what we want for self. We have not been ushered into this place for those things that are simply about selfish gain. We have been brought to this place for kingdom-centered ambitions.

Jesus came to seek and to save that which was lost. God is going to bless us, but God wants us to know that it's about fulfilling His love for people. It's about changing the lives of those that we encounter so that they can change the lives of those that they encounter.

So, to my fellow leaders and entrepreneurs, I encourage you to be the game changer and to be the iron. As we surrender our plan to the ultimate plan, watch God truly multiply your efforts as you model His kingdom by sharing His word in your work.

If your superpower is social media, and you have the capacity to train others to maximize their visibility and do what you do, that is what our Father desires. Yes, we are taking advantage of those gifts and things that God has given us. Yes, it will make us money. Yes, it will bring us before great and mighty men as our gifts are supposed to. Beyond that, it's about changing the game or changing the lives of people to the glory of God. Our bag, gifts and talents are about getting people to the kingdom. It is about pointing individuals to God.

In 2006, Salman Khan started Khan Academy. This Ivy League graduate had spent time working in the technology industry and after graduate school, he worked for an investment firm. While having a conversation with a young cousin who was struggling in math, he agreed to tutor her over the phone and an interactive notepad. Word got out around the family and a number of cousins, nieces, and nephews became students. Sal began to record the sessions and post them on YouTube. They later shared with him that they enjoyed the postings more than the face to face encounters. The recordings provided the ability to pause, rewind, and work at their own pace. Others discovered the videos and began watching as well. He was then connected with Bill Gates and Google … students from around the world are learning mathematics, science, art, and a myriad of other subjects. Khan Academy has been game changing for students of all levels; from your high flyers to special needs and those in the middle. Parents are grateful and students are understanding material that they had previously struggled with. He had no idea this would be the outcome. He saw the need, was compelled to serve, and lives were changed. Our life's work is about being in our God-ordained place to meet the needs of others. What's your game changing shot? What are you holding on to that others need? Salman has created something that has extended far beyond his imagination. Random people just started giving him big money. Who wants to fund that thing that's on the inside of you?

When we look at sports, you hear the word GOAT, the Greatest of All Time. At one time Kareem was thought to be the GOAT, and then Magic Johnson came along and then we had Michael Jordan. All of these men were celebrated for their accomplishments and honored for their greatness. In the Word of God, when it came to being a warrior, David was the greatest of all time. Saul told him to dress in his armor and take on the giant. David refused the king's armor and took the weapons he used while protecting his sheep. He defeated Goliath and would later be celebrated for conquering ten thousand soldiers while Saul had only slayed thousands. Who would have thought that a teenager with a slingshot could bring down a nine-foot giant? It made no sense. Yet we know little becomes much in our Father's hands. When the entire Israeli army hid in fear, David shifted the destiny of two nations because of his reliance on God and submission to His game plan that made him victorious.

My Game Changing Shot

At the end of one year, I joined a Facebook group of women who committed themselves to twenty-one days of corporate prayer and fasting during the month of October. What was to be a twenty-one-day event morphed into something none of us saw coming, including the founder. Out of that one decision, a ministry that always existed inside her fully materialized. It has been amazing to watch. This is what God desires to do with our game changing ***yes!*** He wants us to move on His Word and submit to His direction. Connections have been made as God has taken this person and her followers to places we did not see. Over the course of those next three months we heard the word, we were encouraged to pray, get before God, detox, and to develop our game plan. And we do need to do all those things. But why were we doing it? Because the group ended up morphing into a movement, a ministry, a safe space for women entrepreneurs. Her yes encouraged and positively impacted the lives of so many, including my own, with one simple act of obedience. She'll tell you she didn't know it was going to be like that. I have personally been impacted by her commitment to serving and motivating others. While pushing and pulling me during our coaching relationship, she asked me to do a Facebook live. That thirty-minute conversation resulted in a book, *Her God-Sized Dream*. I never saw it coming, but the lives of many will be changed. What conversation are you having that should be penned and published? What will be your game changing shot?

How do we change our shot?

1. Get started and trust God to complete the work He has started in you. We have to begin the process and follow it through to the end. "Being confident of this very thing, that He who has begun a good work in you will complete it until the day of Jesus Christ; ~Philippians 1:6

2. Get focused: "For the Lord God will help Me; Therefore, I will not be disgraced; Therefore, I have set My face like a flint, And I know that I will not be ashamed. ~ Isaiah 50:7

3. Be Resilient: Just as Kareem encountered and conquered potential setbacks, know that you can too. Stuff will happen, but someone is counting on you to get back up and return to the fight. For a just man falleth seven times, and riseth up again: ~ Pro. 24:16; No temptation has overtaken you except what is common to mankind. And God is faithful; he will not let you be tempted beyond what you can bear. But when you are tempted, he will also provide a way out so that you can endure it. ~ I Corinthians 10:13

4. Get and stay disciplined: Consistency will be our game changer. You'll never change your life until you change something you do daily. The secret of your success is found in your daily routine. ~ John Maxwell.

Prayer:

Heavenly Father, in the name of Jesus, we worship you. We praise you. We magnify your name. We glorify you. God thank you for this year, and thank you for the preparation that has brought us to this point. Thank you, Lord God for all of the online platforms that have brought us together with the common goal of supporting one another to praise You. Thank you for this corporate place of connection.

We have equipped ourselves, but it has not been in our own strength but it's because of who you are in us. And so, God, we surrender every strategy, every plant, every book, every event, every conference. We surrender it to your will, not our plan but your plan. Oh God, thank you for perfecting that which concerns us. What can look like a setback, Father God, it is only a sharpening for those other skills that we have in us. Thank you, Lord God, for shifting us. Thank you for showing us that those things you have placed in us were simply preparations and that at any moment they can be manipulated and reused, Father God. Used in a different way, in a different format God. So, though we have practiced how to dribble, we may need to do a jump shot. Though a layup is normally done in this situation, when the defense does something different, we recognize when we must shift.

We understand that each game is independent of the last and of the one that will come next. So, Father God, we submit every strategy and every plan to you. It is no longer us that lives God, but you. So, we submit our living and our doing to you. We submit our plan and purpose to you. We thank you Father for going before us and making every crooked place straight. We thank you Lord God that we know your voice and the voice of a stranger, we will not follow. We will follow you, Father God.

We live out Proverbs 3:5-6, which says that we are trusting in you with all of our heart, leaning not to our own understanding. In all of our ways we acknowledge you, and you will direct our path. You said the steps of a good man/woman are ordered by you. And so, Father God, we thank you that as we step, we step in you. Father God, we leave fear behind. We leave behind procrastination. We leave behind going around the same mountain, but each moment just as your mercies are new. Every morning we tap into you. We stay hooked into you to get the game plan from the master strategist.

Oh, thank you for all the greatness that shall be done in this year. Yes we have prepared, but Father God, we are just like a pastor who prepares a great message and the moment he steps into the pulpit, you have a different word. Father God, we're ready to change on a dime to please you. We recognize that it is not about us. It is about you, the audience of one. So, we submit ourselves to you. We submit ourselves to your plan. We submit ourselves to your direction, because you are the ultimate gamechanger. You are the greatest of all time, and it is you only who we want to emulate. It is you only who we want to be like and so, Father God, we yield ourselves to be Christians. To be Christ- like, so thank you God for using us. Thank you, God, for the gift. The things that you have placed on the inside of us. We all have different names, and we all have different gifts. And Father God, we will honor the gifts that you have placed on the inside of us, not coveting the gift of those that are around us online, or those on Facebook, because we know that just as our names are different, you've got something specific for each of us to do. Father God, we count ourselves special in you, and blessed that you didn't give us what the other person has. But you gave us exactly what we needed to carry out our purpose that you have selected just for us.

So, Father God, as we said before, we will not compare ourselves with others, but we will thank you for the gift that is us in you. What a gracious father we have. Father God, thank you for gracing us with the power and the ability to walk out, that which you have given to us. We count it a privilege to serve you in this year. We count it a privilege to be an example to those that we encounter. We count it a privilege, Lord God, to propel others to greatness. You have called us to be the leg up. And so, Father, as we are giving and as we are planting, Father God, you are prospering us. So, we need not worry about us, because it's not about us, but it is about you. Therefore, Father, we humbly submit ourselves to you, to your will, your purpose, and your plan. And it is our pleasure, God, to serve you. Thank you, God. I praise, magnify, and exalt your name. And so, Father, we simply say individually, however this shot needs to be made, whatever play needs to be run, we will do it to fulfill your purpose in our lives. We surrender to you, God. We thank you for using us to change the lives of those we will encounter in this season and beyond. Thank you, Father for the privilege of serving you, in Jesus' name, Amen.

Questions for Reflection:

- What is your superpower? What is the thing that God has placed on the inside of you to change the game?
- What plays must you run to get your shot in the basket?
- Who are your teammates and what positions will they play?

Bio

Cheryl Riley has spent the last thirty years of her life developing young people. This was something she never saw coming. Her aspirations were to enter the booming technology field, but God had other plans for this lifelong learner. Just as she was about to graduate college with her Mathematics & Computer Science degree, He called her to the classroom. Little did she know; this would become her professional home and she would enjoy it. Cheryl loves to see the aha lightbulb come on for learners of all ages. Whether it is facilitating a professional development workshop for educators, teaching mathematics to middle and high school students, or ministering to an adult ladies Bible class, teaching is who she is and what she does.

Cheryl has a heart for people and is committed to guiding them to reach their fullest potential in every aspect of life. She and her husband, Alvin, live in Charlotte, NC, and have three adult children. Crystal, Dale, and Jason. **Learn more about Cheryl at cherylcriley.com**

Dare to Believe...

You Are
Worthy, Approved
And
Established

Dare to Believe God, You are Worthy

Roshanda E. Pratt

One of the things I love about our heavenly Father is that where God reveals God heals. That means that whatever God reveals to you over the course of your prayer and devotional times, He wants to heal. It's time out for broken entrepreneurs. It's time out for broken authors who are spilling and bleeding in their published works. We need you to publish works that are going to heal, set free and deliver people. It's time out for creatives not to be able to fully manifest the gift of God in their life, because there are places in their lives where they still need healing. There's no shame; we all have places that we need God to heal. One of the ways to start that healing process is daring to believe God that you are worthy.

Dare to Believe God, You Are Worthy

In 2 Timothy 2:20 – 22 it says, "Now in a large house there are not only vessels and objects of gold and silver, but also vessels and objects of wood and of earthenware, and some are for honorable (noble, good) use and some for dishonorable (ignoble, common). Therefore, if anyone cleanses himself from these things [which are dishonorable—disobedient, sinful], he will be a vessel for honor, sanctified [set apart for a special purpose and], useful to the Master, prepared for every good work. Run away from youthful lusts—pursue righteousness, faith, love, and peace with those [believers] who call on the Lord out of a pure heart." (Amplified)

This is a year for you to determine and walk in the worthiness that God has called upon you; to walk in the worthiness that God has placed on the inside of you. You do not need to let your worth be determined by how much money you have or don't have. God has called you worthy since the beginning, and now it is time for you to walk in it. Your worth should not be determined by what circles you are part of or what circles you're not invited to join. It should not be determined by someone's filter on Instagram, and certainly do not let your worth be determined by how many likes you get on a Facebook live. However, your worth is determined by the worth God has assigned to you as both an individual, entrepreneur, author, and creative. Decide to let your worth be determined by God's worth today.

As an entrepreneur, I have heard this phrase, "I am going to charge people what I am worth. They're going to pay me what I am worth. No longer are people going to pick my brain, they are going to pay me what I am worth." But those statements are flawed because it implies that I am a certain dollar figure. It implies if someone pays me $10,000, that's what I am worth. If I am paid $1.2 million, that is what I am worth. I know what you are trying to say, but it is flawed in theory. The theory causes my worthiness to be capped like a salary. However, when we look at what Christ Jesus did for us, the fact God loved us so much He sent his only begotten Son to die for us. When we see what Jesus did on the cross, when we see that He paid a debt, too much for me to pay. Not only did He pay my debt, but He endowed me with gifts like speaking, writing, and a business acumen. I can assign a dollar amount on the solutions I provide, but I could never ever assign a value on the cost of my life.

2 Timothy 2:20-22, discusses two kinds of vessels, both carrying different worth. You have a vessel of honor. Here is an analogy, you can either be a fine china or a paper plate. Fine china cannot go into the dishwasher, because it's delicate and will break. However, a paper plate can be discarded. You don't treat it with honor or respect. What is amazing about this journey of entrepreneurship is that I have the ability to decide how I will show up every day. Fine china used for honorable use or a

paper plate, one for common use. Dare to believe God, you are worthy! You are worthy of being a vessel of honor.

3 Ways You Can Start Daring to Believe God You are Worthy:

1. **Make a decision:** There is so much power in a decision. Decide you will be used for honorable use. That begins by stepping from the background into the forefront. Decide this is the year you are going to show up. Every day, by your actions, you are deciding if you will be a vessel of honor or one of common use. You are worthy of coming out of the background and being a hidden figure. You are worthy of putting out your written works. You are worthy of showing the world your creativity, because God gave it to you. You are worthy of being an entrepreneur and doing things honorably in God's way, because you are His chosen vessel. It is your decision.

2. **Lay aside the weight:** Put aside the thing that's coming between you fully manifesting as the vessel of honor. For example, one of the things I often talk about as a live video strategist is that it's your mandate as a messenger to make sure that when you're speaking to people, that you're speaking from a healed place and not a broken place. This helps you to get on a platform such as live video, or any platform for that matter, and ensure you're not bleeding on people, but you're healing people. Laying aside every weight means you walk in forgiveness; you walk in wholeness; and you deal with the *pink* elephant in the room. For me the pink elephant was dealing with my inconsistency and my lack of discipline. Before I got serious about my health, God was telling me, your wealth and your health are connected. He said, "How you treat your money is how you treat your health." Maybe you are how I used to be, sporadic, sometimes you're on it and sometimes you're not. Sometimes you look at the numbers and sometimes you don't. So, I had to lay aside every weight and deal with my own pink elephant, my inconsistency.

You have to decide that you're going to be a vessel of honor and not a common object. You have to decide what your role is in this family and this Kingdom of God's assignment is. If you decide to be common, that's okay. That's your decision. Scripture tells us that choose ye this day who you will serve. Every day we're making a choice about if we're going to be a vessel of honor or a vessel that's common. However, there's nothing common about Jesus Christ and I don't want to be common. I want to be a vessel that He can use to serve people well. When you have the president coming to your house, you're not giving him paper plates. When you have a nice dinner and you're welcoming people to your house, you pull out the nice stuff for people to eat off of, right? Why? Because you're showing them that you honor them. Are you showing people I honor you; I respect you, and I want to pull out my nice stuff for you and not my paper plate? You have to decide today I'm going to lay aside the weight, and you have to decide today that I'm going to be a vessel of honor and no longer just common.

We serve a God who's extraordinary. He's bad and I'm not talking about bad like the regular definition. I'm talking about bad like the kids said, "He's bad to the bone." That means He's wonderful; He's altogether lovely; and He's amazing. Why? Because He created the world from nothing. He took chaos and brought cosmos to it. That's pretty bad stuff. And the same presence of Christ Jesus who did that is living on the inside of you. That means I can't be common, average, or ordinary. It means I have to get average out of my mind and go to being extraordinary. What is the thing that God is calling you to lay aside and deal with?

3. **Honor God:** Jade Simmons, a fellow co-author in this book, blessed me with her message on focusing on God being your first client. As an entrepreneur, author, and as a creative, create places in your business or endeavors where you are honoring God. For example, I have received several inbox messages from millennial women who want

mentorship. I decided I would take time every quarter to pour back into these women. This is not about payment or creating another stream of income, but seeking the Kingdom of God first. Put first things first. I know that when I put God's ministry first, He will take care of everything else. Scripture promises us that when we seek ye first the Kingdom of God and his righteousness, everything else will be added.

What is the project, or what I like to call purpose projects, that God has been speaking to you about that you have not done yet? Why haven't you done it? Most times we don't do it because we are caught up in common things like, "Oh, I don't have enough money to meet my needs." But as a person who spent the first part of her life broken, I now understand how God gives you beauty for ashes. The healing you need to manifest in your life comes from sowing in someone else's. When you're faithful over someone else's stuff, God can be faithful over yours. So instead of being focused so much on what you have to do, focus on how you can be an honorable vessel? You may ask again, how can I be an honorable vessel? It is because you are worthy. You are going to lay aside the weight and decide that you're going to be an honorable vessel that God can use. You're not going to be common or average any longer. You're going to be committed to doing that thing that God told you to do, even if you're not on the winning side of it. Even if you're not getting money from it, getting exposure, being in the circle or getting an award for it, you're going to do what your God has asked you to do and be committed to that.

Prayer to Believe Your Worth

Father, in the name of Jesus, I pray for every entrepreneur, every author, and every creative. I pray in the name of Jesus, that they understand the worth of God that's upon their life. I know in past times they may have not felt worthy. I know in past times they may have faced challenges and it was tough. They may have had to deal with circumstances and situations where people made them feel like they were less than or made them feel like they're not worthy, that may have treated them like they were common. But Father, they're rising up and they're discovering that they are worthy, not because of their works, not because of the circles they hang in, but because of what Jesus Christ did for them on Calvary: What Jesus Christ did through the shedding of his blood and what He did through the resurrection.

So Father, in the name of Jesus, raise up your sons and daughters and have them take their rightful place. The whole of creation is moaning and yearning for them to show up worthy as vessels of honor that can be used for your kingdom and to tear down the kingdom of darkness when it comes to business, when it comes to published works, when it comes to the media, and when it comes to creativity. Father, I pray in Jesus' name, that they realize that they are worthy, and they show up like that in the name of Jesus. Father, I'm asking you to even go into their mind and those places of things they remember as a child or when people spoke negatively about them. Father, demolish those things, the words that didn't produce life that were spoken over their lives, and the things that they saw or witnessed that goes against the vessel you have created them to be. I pray that you go before them Father, and you go in their mind and you start to strip away those things.

Thank you for what you've already revealed in their life and that they show up and they deal with those things God. Because at the end of the day, Lord, you have a great place for us and it is a big vision God. Everything that we're doing is just building upon where you're taking us in the years ahead. Father, I pray in Jesus' name, they'll no longer show up as common, but they'll show up and say, "Here I am Lord. I'm your vessel of honor and you can use me", in Jesus' name. Amen

Say these declarations with me:
> I declare I am worthy, because God says I am
> I declare I am a person of honor.
> I declare my business is honorable.

Dare to believe you are worthy.

Questions for Reflection:
- What has God revealed about your value?
- What gifts/talents do you have that can make the world better?
- What must you do to bring those gifts/talents out?

Bio

Roshanda E. Pratt, known online as The "Rosho" Live is a media pioneer merging her 20 years' experience as a Television News Producer and Social Media Influencer to equip brands, businesses, and thought leaders to amplify their voice and monetize their story both on air and online. She's author of the best-selling book, *CEO of Live Video*, and her call is to raise up messengers who will use the power of media to impact the world. **Learn more about RoShanda at www.therosholive.com**

Dare to Believe God, You Are Approved

Melissa J. Nixon

Confidence has never been something I've dealt with, but there have been certain things in my life where I have sought approval for things. When I took my leap over five years ago, I've always known that I was called to be on stages and coach people. It's my gift and I don't have an issue with saying that. I know that anyone can call me right now and their audience will leave changed.

But even with confidence and over 5 years of living the dream I said I wanted, there was something still missing in my life and in this journey. One Fall, I prayed to God that I wanted a business that uses all of me. I wanted a business where I didn't just do a training where people were only inspired for a day. I felt like there was something. I've always been a woman of faith. People who have followed me for any significant amount of time via social media and on my email list have known that, but there was still something missing. The missing part was me not being afraid of incorporating publicly who I am as a woman of faith and publicly praying out loud … essentially a more public ministry.

Many of my private corporate and business clients chose me because of my faith. However, they did not know that prayer was my gift. Their reactions were always priceless and ranged anywhere from joy to thankfulness. And while prayer has been my secret weapon in business, I've known that prayer was a gift of mine long before I had a business. Before my dad went to heaven he would always say, "Baby, you know how to get a prayer through." At one point, he was in a phase where he had walked away from God for a little while. He would say, "Daughter, I need you to pray for me because you know how to get a prayer through."

Beyond Inspiration

At the time I didn't know what that meant. I just knew I knew how to pray and talk to God. From there I would begin to pray with my friends and family. I would pray at work whenever there was a disaster or a team member was in a time of need. I always knew the one thing we needed to do was pray. Then I started my business and it was this secret sauce I had that you only knew about if you worked with me. If you were a private client, we would start and end their calls in prayer. And if they were going through something *big*, we would close out in intercessory prayer.

But like you, there have been certain things I have ran from throughout my life and ministry is one of them. I didn't want to necessarily be associated with it. I was all about business. Plus, I did not know how to make money praying. I didn't know how to make money in ministry, therefore I wanted and needed to be about business. I needed to go after six figure contracts in corporate. But even with all the business savviness, corporate contracts, speaking engagements, and coaching clients there was still something missing from my life and business.

The Fall I prayed and told God that I wanted Him to use all of me is also when my good friend Jade asked me, "When will you finally surrender? When will you finally stop running?" She asked, "What is it that scares you about ministry? Well, that weekend was the weekend I did a lot of soul searching, finally surrendered, and finally found the thing I had been missing. The very next thing I did was take what used to be my very private prayers with my private clients and shared my gift of prayer publicly. At the time, I was going through some things in my business and battling all kinds of thoughts and emotions. I knew I could not be the only one going through ups and downs, but that is surely how the enemy would make me feel. I became discontent with just sharing inspirational posts, posts about God, and posts about prayer. That is when God said I need you to pray for 21 days, not just by myself, but online …on Facebook.

I said yes, but I definitely felt some kind of way with a certain level of nervousness. I honestly asked myself, "Who am I to do that?" That is when God began to deal with me about it and I heard Him say, "You are already pre-approved." That is what I need you to know about anything you feel called to that seems bigger than you and you ask yourself that same question. The answer is still the same, you are already pre-approved. When God has called you to something, no one has to put their stamp of approval on it or on you, because you are already predestined. It doesn't matter if no one else is doing it, you are the first to do it, or if everyone is doing it. God still called *you* to do it too. You're already pre-approved. So, I took my pre-approved self and prayed for 21 days with an online community that grew over a 1000 people in less than a month. God literally blew our minds during that month and has continued to do so ever since. That prayer community then became our online Facebook community – Prayers, Promises, and Profits. During that time of prayer that month, God said, "I need you to pray on New Year's Day not for 30 min, not for an hour but for hours. I knew that I was supposed to kick-off the year in prayer!

I need you to know something about prayer. Prayer *is* the thing that changes things, but the one thing I've had to grow in is that I've had to believe what I've prayed. I've had to elevate my prayers. I've had to elevate my faith. I've had to be able to see myself as God sees me and see God as God. I had to stop praying little baby prayers and start praying the promises of God over my life. I had to stop doing what I had been "taught" about business building in the coaching industry and always having an offer or an upsell, and just pray big prayers. I had to pray big prayers not only for myself but for others who desperately need it too.

Sometimes you just need to walk in obedience. What people witnessed in my life and business during and since that 21 days of prayer was not just a confident Melissa, but a nervous one who learned she was already pre-approved and predestined by God. The Amplified Version of Ephesians 1:3 talks about the blessings of redemption. It says,

Beyond Inspiration

> *"Blessed and worthy of praise be the God and father of Lord Jesus Christ who blessed us with every spiritual blessing in the heavenly realms in Christ just as in His love, He chose us in Christ before the foundation of the world ..."*

It did not happen when some influencer said you're ready, your coach says you're ready, your best friend says you're ready, or when your parents say you're ready but before the foundation of the world.

> *"... So that we would be holy and blameless in his sight. In love. He predestined and loving planned for us to be adopted to himself as his own children through Jesus Christ in accordance with the kind intention and good pleasure of his will to the praise of his glorious grace and favor, which he so freely bestowed on us in the beloved. In Him we have redemption through his blood, the forgiveness and complete pardon of our sin in accordance with the riches of His grace, which he lavished on us in all wisdom and understanding He made known to us the mystery of his will according to his good pleasure, which he purposed in Christ with regard to the fulfillment of the times to bring all things together in Christ, things in the heavens and things on the earth. In Him also we have received an inheritance, having been predestined according to the purpose of Him who works everything in agreement with the counsel and design of His will, so that we who were the first to hope in Christ [who first put our confidence in Him as our Lord and Savior] would exist to the praise of His glory. In Him, you also, when you heard the word of truth, the good news of your salvation, and believed in Him, were stamped with the seal of the promised Holy Spirit as owned and protected.* Ephesians 1: 4 - 13

Now the question is do you believe you were predestined before the foundation of the world or are you waiting to be pre-approved by someone to do what God has called you to do? You have the gifts. The things that are in you, both the gifts and the desire for what's ahead are not new. In fact, not only did God place them inside of you, but He already knew what their intended use was for. It's just that *you* are just now finding out about it. You are finally recognizing what's inside of you, who you are, and who's you are. Once I recognized who I was and who's I was, my whole life changed. Once you realize you are pre-approved and do not need anyone else's approval, your life will change too. Your year will change, your family, and your career/business will change. You don't need the approval of anyone to do anything, because you have already been predestined.

This is not a numbers game

This is not a numbers game. Social media and influencers will make you believe that it's a numbers game and we have to have a certain amount of likes on our pages, or that we have to have a certain amount of views on our video, or even a certain amount of money in the bank. All of that is coming, but sometimes you have to recognize your pre-approval status before the numbers even come. Sometimes the numbers don't come until you recognize your pre-approval status in the Kingdom, because you're trying to do it the world's way and not God's way. God said, I predestined you before the world was born, not when so and so liked or shared your posts. Nor was your approval validated when they invited you on their show or asked you, "Can you blog for me?" You were predestined even before any of those acknowledgements. It's okay to get excited. It's okay when someone signs up for your coaching program, but if nobody signs up, you're still predestined, still pre-approved.

In everyday life, we have a number of things we have to be pre-approved for such as a car loan, house loan, and more. During that process they look at everything to see if you qualify. They look at your background, your credit, they determine how much you're worth, and then they give you a sheet of paper or an email that states your value and whether or not you are preapproved. That piece of paper or email is like money in the bank. If you are in the market for a house, it's money in the bank because you can take it to any realtor and it basically says you can afford this amount of house. Guess what? You already had your pre-approval papers before the foundation of the world. The best part about it is that it's not limited to the amount of a house or the amount of a car. Your pre-approval papers are unlimited in the kingdom.

It's the same way we get better interest rates if we belong to certain banks. For example, if you're a part of a credit union you can get better interest rates for personal, home, and car loans than a traditional bank. But guess what? Before the foundation of the world, you were already a part of the best credit union there ever was and ever will be. You are already pre-approved.

The God-size ideas you have do not need to be signed off by anyone. You only need to run it by God Himself. Why? Because He's the one who gave it to you in the first place. Instead of waiting on others, overthinking it, or perfecting it … don't delay, run with it. The times I ran with the voice of God and did the things that He placed in my heart like the 21 days of prayer for entrepreneurs, or 12 hours of prayer on New Year's Day, the gratitude expressed by those who participated was endless. But here's the thing for both instances and more, I didn't get permission from anyone to do it. Once I realized I was pre-approved, I started moving. While I love all who support me and cheer me on and respect those who say don't do it or say no to opportunities, I have to move forward anyway. Why? Because it was a God said moment, not a people said moment. Don't miss your God said moment, because you were waiting on someone else's approval of yourself or your idea. Don't let your God said moments happen 3 or 5 years from now, because you were waiting on your numbers to tick up or to be seen or accepted by certain crowds. You were accepted even before you were conceived in your mother's womb.

The reason prayer is so essential is because there are so many people full of gifts, full of opportunity, and full of the anointing, but they don't get fully leveraged because you don't know who you are in the kingdom. I guarantee once you get your position right, once you know you already have your pre-approval letter that is like a blank check because it's unlimited, there is no lid. There is no cap. Your life, your business, and your ministry will change extraordinarily.

Melissa J. Nixon

Prayer:

Father God, I thank you for drawing people back to the heart of you through prayer. I thank you that in this burst of entrepreneurship that is taking place over the last few years, and where your own sons and daughters have chased after people, they will now chase after you. They've chased after coaches, but they now chase after you. They felt like they haven't been adequate enough, that they haven't been equipped because they don't know enough, but I thank you that through prayer you will download divine revelation of what to do in their business. You will download divine revelation of who to talk to, who to call, what next steps to take. You will show them who will be their coach, who will be their mentor, who will be their business bestie. You will give them divine alignment with who they are supposed to be connected to.

I thank you that you are raising up not just women and men of faith, but you are raising up warriors in the kingdom that will literally go to battle with the enemy and come against anything that is unlike you. That we will be the ones on the front lines. I thank you that there will be an acceleration of faith-based businesses in every single industry. I pray for your business. If you're in the government industry, I pray for your business. If you are in the finance industry, I pray for Your business. If you are an author, I pray for your business. If you are in retail, I pray for your business. Have you been in media? I thank you that you are raising up Kingdom men and women to go into the marketplace to be the new thing, to do the new thing. I thank you that you will literally take the lid off of these businesses, because they have stopped chasing everything else and they have come back to that first love. I thank you that this will be the year that we won't chase anything but you. We will only chase after you in 2019; we won't chase money.

We won't chase numbers; we will chase you. As we seek ye first the Kingdom of Heaven, everything else will be added unto you, in the name of Jesus. I thank you God that you are unleashing God ideas for the year ahead. I thank you where they've been held back by fear that they will be so full of faith that you will literally say fear has to go. Even if they move in spite of fear, they will trust you more than the fear that they have. I thank you God that we will no longer be ashamed. We will no longer run. We will no longer hide. We will no longer be a hidden figure, but we would stand bold and proud of the gifts and the calling that you gave us. We would be audacious.

We would be recklessly bold. When people say you are acting different, you would already know the reason why. You will be able to realize it's because you are a child of the king. The world will no longer make fun of believers in business saying that we're flaky, saying that all we do is pray about stuff. But Lord, I thank you that we will pray and we will implement. We will implement and see God results. They will look and want to know what the strategy is. They will look and want to know how to move forward. Father, we thank you that you are doing a shift now amongst kingdom businesses. You are doing a shift amongst women of faith and we will no longer be timid. We will no longer have to go and pray hours for things and have nothing to show for it. We will be the lender and not the borrower. We will be the head and not the tail. We will be the one sitting, invited at the table with things and ideas that everyone needs, in the name of Jesus.

Father, I thank you God. I seal everything that they've read throughout this book. I thank you that whatever anyone got from this devotional will not be snatched back by the enemy. I thank you for reminding them how when they worshipped you in the past the ideas you gave them and will give them are already pre-approved by you. Father we thank you, we love you, and we bless your name. In Jesus' name, Amen.

Questions for Reflection:

- What areas of your life or career will have more greater impact and influence because you full understanding that you are pre-destined and pre-approved?

- Pick one of those areas and share more in depth what your impact and influence would look like if there was no hesitation or delay.
- While the vision God gave you may be more than you can comprehend at times, what are one or two things you know or feel in your spirit God is leading you to do now?

Bio

Melissa J. Nixon ***prepares, positions, and pushes*** leaders and organizations to make their next courageous move. The "Courage Coach", as she is called, is known for being a thought-driver and the keynote speaker that will do more than be inspiring. She challenges audiences everywhere to own their voice, show up more powerfully, and live by her motto, "I'm not afraid of failure, I am afraid of regret!"

The energy she brings to every stage causes a change in the lives of the audiences. She re-energizes them and breaks down perceived barriers in their thinking. Simple, practical, and real-life scenarios keep audiences engaged and ready to return and take action. There's sure to be laughter, ah-ha moments, and "Yes I can!" revelations. Yes, your audience will be pushed to show up every day as their most courageous self.

She is also the author of The Courageous Life - How to Leap from Your Career to Your Calling and The Profit Playbook for Women – The Ultimate Resource Guide for Building a Successful Business. **Learn more about Melissa at melissajnixon.com.**

Established in Prayer

Otescia R. Johnson

"Forever O Lord, Your word is settled in heaven. Your faithfulness endures to all generations; You established the earth, and it abides. They continue this day according to Your ordinances, for all are Your servants." – Psalm 119:89-91 (NKJV)

One of the messages that the Lord always deals with me very heavily about, as it pertains to my business, is the fact that being an entrepreneur was not just something I decided to do. Walking in entrepreneurship is an answer to a mandate from Heaven. God called me to entrepreneurship. With that in mind, I consistently remind myself that this is not just something I decided to do on my own, but it's something I do according to the leading of the Holy Spirit. If I know God is leading me to do something, then I can't make decisions on my own. I must make all decisions according to what the Lord is telling me to do. I must establish my business in prayer because it began as a spiritual instruction.

When God gives us instructions, He releases His word concerning the matter. As the scripture listed above states, the entire earth is held together by the word of God. If the world is established and sustained by His word, why would we doubt God's ability to establish and sustain us in business? I want to share my personal experiences with you to prove that God is still in the business of sustaining everything He instructs us to do, but it must first be established in prayer.

In 2011, I thought my life was great. I was working for a company I loved. I had co-workers I respected and genuinely enjoyed being around. My personal life was absolutely fantastic as money flowed well, my husband and I were enjoying raising our lively clan, and we had a church family we adored. Everything seemed to be going extremely well. Then one day as I was driving to an event for work, the Lord posed this question to me, "Do you trust me?" The question seemed innocuous at the time, but it was far from innocent. It was the catalyst of a multi-year journey of establishment that ultimately led to me being a part of this powerful book. After assuring the Lord that I trusted Him emphatically, He gave me the following instruction, "Don't get comfortable on this job. You won't be here long." I was taken aback by His words, but as I stated, I trusted Him, so I simply said, "okay."

Over the next year and half, I began to find fault with so many things concerning my job. Small things that never bothered me before started irritating me. I found myself praying on the way to work just so I'd be fortified enough to get through the day. I started dreaming about storylines and writing to release stress. The more I wrote, the less I enjoyed my job. Then it happened, I received a phone call from our corporate office. Despite all of our success, I was told my office would be closed immediately. I was asked to pack up my office and vacate the premises right away. Initially, I was excited. I sort of felt it coming so I'd removed most of my personal items from my office. It took me less than 10 minutes to pack up the few remaining items and head home. I called my husband and informed him and we both rejoiced. I was relieved to finally be done. However, as soon as the dust settled, the severance ended, and our savings ran out, I found myself feeling completely distraught. I asked God if I should look for another job and He gave me a stern, "NO". He told me to trust Him. The prior conversation I'd had with Him came rushing back. Yes, I trusted Him, but the mounting stress and fear of the unknown was beginning to overwhelm me. I went to church one afternoon and cried out to Him,

"I don't know how to do this. How do I help my husband provide for our family without getting a job? Whose life can I study? Where is the blueprint?"

He quickly replied, "I am the blueprint. Trust me to walk you through this."

Beyond Inspiration

Over the next few years, God and I settled into a rhythm. I asked Him what to do, He gave me instructions, and I remained faithful to praying for the when, how, and where of the matter. Every time God told me to trust Him, I knew He was going to establish something new in and through me. When He told me to launch my business, I was initially hesitant for all of the typical reasons. However, because of how He'd proven Himself to me in everything else, I obeyed Him and took the leap. The results have been far beyond anything I thought or imagined. Not only has God taught me how to steward the business He told me to start, He has led me to create new programs and courses that are helping other Kingdom Entrepreneurs walk out their call to entrepreneurship.

As a Kingdom Entrepreneur you must understand your first call is back to relationship with God and radical obedience to His every instruction. As you walk uprightly before Him, He establishes you in the earth. As His children, we cannot simply do what everyone else is doing in business. We were never called to fit in with the world, we were called to have dominion over it. We have been given the spiritual authority to operate as His agents here in the earth. Instead of following the status quo, we're called to correct a corrupted standard. Instead of bending the rules to make an extra dollar, we're called to follow Heaven's rules AND live in supernatural abundance. The way of the world is to do whatever it takes to increase profits year over year, the way of the Kingdom is to seek God's guidance on how to establish and grow what He's called us to lead. Your business is a for-profit extension of your personal ministry. For it to be successful, you cannot ignore the ministry side of what you do. Whether it's praying with your clients, or offering pro bono services, God called you into entrepreneurship so that through your influence you can be His hands, feet, and mouthpiece in the marketplace. You have the solution to someone's problem on the inside of you. You may have wondered your whole life why you don't seem to fit in with anyone around you. It's because you were not called to fit in with them, you were called to lead them. You are called to be a leader in your industry, a forerunner who establishes a legacy for generations to come. As you increase your prayer life, you increase your effectiveness within the earth.

When you are looking to make the shift from simply establishing your business in prayer to seeing the physical manifestation of what you've been praying for, it is important to begin releasing declarations. Declarations are simply you utilizing the authority God has given you to command the Earth realm to come into alignment with what has already been established in Heaven. I am going to share some of my personal declarations with you that have changed my life both personally and professionally. I pray you will use your God-given dominion to release these declarations over your life and business so that you can see what you have established in prayer manifested in the natural.

Before you read the declarations, I want to dispel the one lie that keeps so many Kingdom Entrepreneurs from seeing what they are praying for. It is the lie that has been around since the days of Adam and Eve. It is the lie of, "Did God really say that?" It is imperative that you do not allow this small, but impactful question to nag you and sow seeds of doubt in what you are about to decree. When the enemy asked Eve this question, he undermined her belief in God's word and ultimately seduced her into disobeying God. (Genesis 3:1) His tricks do not change. He is still robbing God's children of their inheritance by simply asking,

"Did God really say that? Did God really call you to entrepreneurship? Did God really tell you to move to that city? Did God really tell you to marry that person?"

If we aren't careful, we can be pulled into a vicious cycle of doubt, unbelief, and self-flagellation. This gives the enemy an open door to your thoughts and allows him to continue to sow his lies right next to the truth. After a while, the lies begin to spread like weeds in a garden and it becomes difficult to determine where truth ends, and the lie begins. You'll start convincing yourself you didn't hear God correctly. Instead of launching one product that brings in 6 figures like God promised, you'll start trying to launch five mini products because the lie of the enemy made you believe that would have a higher conversion rate. The enemy wants you to work hard for the same results God wants to *GIVE* to you.

Remember, you were never intended to work to provide for yourself. You were created to obey God as He provides for you. Your business is simply a resource He uses to funnel money to you, but God is your ultimate source. The Bible states in Philippians 4:19 that God shall supply all of your needs. When we understand provision, we let go of the world's system of working our fingers to the bone for every little morsel and we embrace the Kingdom system of listening to the voice of God and following His directions to success. The doubt the enemy throws your way is purposed to rob you of the reward that is on the other side of your diligent obedience. That's why he tries to trick you into believing you didn't hear God correctly. He wants you to disobey so you'll miss out on what God has already pre-destined for you to have.

What you have to understand is, every time you hear:

"What if God didn't really say that? Maybe you should consider doing this differently. What if you can't do it?"

Anytime you think those thoughts, you know they are lies from the enemy. His number one trick is to convince you that you did not hear God correctly. It is the same lie that he used on Eve in the garden, and he still uses that exact same lie today.

- What if you heard God wrong?
- What if you're mistaken?
- What if this fails?

It's the number one thing that he uses to keep you from moving forward as God has ordained. Instead of entertaining his lies, I learned to lay before God and ask Him,

"God, what does this business need to look like? Who am I called to help? Who am I called to serve? Whose life is intended to be enriched through this business?"

Notice I didn't question the validity of the business or entertain the lie of "maybe I shouldn't be doing this." Instead I went straight to the source of my inspiration and trusted my ability to hear His voice. His sheep know His voice and follow Him! (John 10:27)

Now that we have dispelled doubt and the lies of the enemy, let's dive into the declarations that have shifted my life and business! Pray them aloud so that your sound is released in the earth.

Declarations

The winds have begun to change and now revenue is finding me from the north, the south, the east, and the west.

I decree and declare that in the name of Jesus, Otescia Johnson *(insert your name or the name of your business here)* is a household name, not for my glory, but for the glory of the Lord.

Everyone who comes in contact with me will be enriched. Their lives will be greatly blessed because they have interacted with me.

Everything that I put my hands to begins to prosper. I will consistently see quarter over quarter growth in my business. I will see more money in my lifetime than anybody in the history of my bloodline. My children are generationally blessed because of the work that I put forth in this business on today.

I have enough hours in the day. I have enough time to sleep and enough time to work. I have enough time to be a mother and enough time to be a wife. I have enough time to be a minister and enough time to be a student. I have enough time to spend alone with God and enough time to release His word. I have enough time to do everything that God calls me to do.

I am not overwhelmed by new clients as they come into my business, but I am blessed by the influx of responsibility and the influx of revenue that comes into my hands.

I am one whose hands are readily open to give because just the same way that my hands are open to give out, they're open for God to flow more into them, in the name of Jesus.

My words have power and the Earth realm has no choice but to line up with the words that come out of my mouth.

I don't bend to what I see, but what I see bends according to my words.

I am not controlled by Earth's limitations, but the Earth is controlled by what I say. I don't care what I see or what it looks like. If there's a mountain, it needs to get out of my way.

I go to Heaven and I get strategies. The strategies that I get from Heaven dictate what happens here in the Earth realm.

The oil of the Lord flows through me, and it blesses everywhere that I dwell.

I am a person who carries increase within my belly and the increase of the Lord is what dictates what goes on around me, in Jesus' name.

I am the chosen one of Israel, and I have been anointed to set an entire generation free.

I have been raised to heavenly places, seated with Jesus Christ.

I am the influencer of the influencers, and because of the power of God that is on the inside of me, we are influencing an entire culture of people.

We are reclaiming the culture for Jesus.

The effects of my work in the Earth will never cease to be felt, in Jesus' name.

He will increase my visibility. The more people that see me… the more people that will see Him.

The more people that lay eyes on me, the more people that will know there is a true and living God who has their best interests at heart. They will understand that God is a God that cannot lie and everything that He says, it shall come to pass.

The people will know that He is a rewarder of those that diligently seek Him.

I declare that because I diligently seek Him, God is consistently rewarding me every day.

I expect to see the reward of the Lord, for expectation is the foundation of my destiny. As I add to my expectation, righteous living, God begins to manifest my destiny in ways that I never imagined. He begins to flow through me in ways that I could not see.

Through my prayer life, power is added unto me. Through my prayer life, I'm a giant in the kingdom. Through my prayer life, other people are transformed. Through my prayer life, my business grows. I have been given dominion over the Earth. It is through my prayer life that victory is won. I don't have to fight and toil in the natural because I established things in heaven and as I establish things in heaven, the God of all creation can cause the earth realm to come into alignment.

The Earth realm does not have free choice. I decree to the Earth: You have no other option than to yield your increase. You have no other choice but to do that which God has decreed. You have no other choice but to follow the words that come out of my mouth.

I have authority in the Earth realm. It is through this authority that I can take captive everything that goes against the word of God. It is through this authority that I can move and flow according to the heavenly realms.

I don't sound like anyone else. I don't try to look like anyone else. I don't try to move the way that anyone else moves, but I move according to the Holy Spirit alone. It is through my obedience to Him that He has carved out my own special place within the marketplace.

It is through my authenticity, my uniqueness, my quirkiness, and all the idiosyncrasies of me, that God reaches down into the soul of somebody else and He adds a blessing unto them.

It is through me being all of who God created me to be that lives are being transformed, that generational healing begins to happen.

I decree and declare that everywhere I travel, I release the word of the Lord, and the word of the Lord over that region begins to grow and then begins to manifest the thing that God has called it to do, in the name of Jesus.

It is what happens behind closed doors that makes all the difference in the lives of the strangers that I pray for.

It is through my voice that everything sent by the enemy is destroyed and the only thing that will go forward is the word of the Lord, in Jesus' name.

The declarations you just read are powerful statements that I heard during prayer. I released what I heard, and God established it. Because my business was established in prayer and not established by Otescia, God has a responsibility to care for it. Every single thing that God creates, He assumes responsibility over. If you're praying for anything in your business, please know it must first be established in heaven. The Lord's prayer in the 6th chapter of Matthew instructs us regarding how to pattern our prayer…. on Earth, as it is in Heaven. If you have not first established a thing in Heaven, there will be nothing to manifest on Earth. It won't work any other way. Once you establish a thing in Heaven, you can call forth manifestation in the Earth. All of your success begins and ends with Heaven.

For those of you walking in fear because you tried to start a business before and it didn't seem to work, you've tried to launch a book and it wasn't successful, or you've tried to launch a ministry and it failed, don't worry, you're in good company. Many of those you follow on social media and in real life have had similar experiences. Falling down is simply an opportunity to get up again. Do not allow fear of failure to hold you hostage. Instead of being paralyzed into stagnation, I want you to go back to God and ask Him the questions listed below so that He can guide you to the success He has planned for you. Remember, God will show you how to manifest what you establish in prayer.

Questions for Reflection:
- How do I establish what You have called me to?
- What needs to change in order for me to see the manifestation of Your promises?
- How can I use what You establish through me, to make life better for someone else?

Bio:

Otescia R. Johnson is a skilled writer, ordained Prophetess, captivating and innovative speaker, bestselling author, and consummate entrepreneur. She is the founder of O. Johnson Ministries, the Healing the Hurt Women's Conference, and B.O.Y. Enterprises, Inc, as well as the creator of the *Magnetize Your Life* and *Roadmap to Publication* systems.

Otescia's greatest joy is empowering the masses to wake up every day to bet on themselves. She accomplishes this through keynote addresses, workshop facilitation, publications, conferences, and one-on-one coaching. As the founder of multiple businesses and ministries, Otescia uses her experience in the worlds of business and faith to help believers merge their passions as they navigate the journey of entrepreneurship. When she isn't empowering the masses, Otescia enjoys spending her days soaking up the laughter of her husband and children. **Learn more about Otescia by visiting otesciajohnson.com**

Dare to Believe…

You Are Prepared for the Next Level!

How to Pray for Your Next Level from the Inside Out

Saundra Wall Williams

Next Level... How many times have you heard someone say, "I'm ready for my next level?" Maybe you have said, "I'm going to my next level", at one time or another. I know that I have spoken next level to myself and others have spoken it to me but there was still something missing. I often said these words about where I desired to go, but for reasons unknown to me at the time, I could not get there. I wanted to see next level in my career, ministry, and business. Therefore, I began to pray for the missing roadmap to get me there. What follows is my story, God's Divine revelation through scripture, the strategy to next level, and a prayer for your next level.

My Story

I had the "perfect career", but it was not enough. I was the Senior Vice President for the third largest Community College System in the world. I wanted more because I knew there was a next level for me. My desire was to create a business that would replace the six-figure income I had as a Senior Vice President and allow me to live the abundant life that was promised to me in John 10:10,

> *"I am come that they might have life, and that they might have it more abundantly."*

It was time for Next Level

I was working at least 60 hours per week. It seems unbelievable but that was my reality. My mind and thoughts seemed to always be on something that was work related. I enjoyed what I did and loved the people I worked with, but at the same time I knew there was more. God had a higher calling and profession for me where I would operate completely in my purpose.

Before coming to community colleges, I worked in the area of technology with three major technology companies. While I enjoyed the work and I continuously learned from every position I held, I knew I needed to shift to get to my next level. Each time I moved positions, I thought I was going to that infamous "next level" when in reality I was only changing jobs. While at community colleges, I realized that what I was learning in my day to day job helped me in the work outside of the office. I was a high profile, award winning leader in technology. The leadership skills, experiences, and resources I amassed from thirty-two years of corporate, education, and government leadership positioned me to coach, consult, mentor, and develop other women in leadership both professionally and personally. I had acquired a unique body of knowledge, skills, and abilities that were transferable to my own business, ministry, and other organizational work. But before I go on, let me ask you this question. Are there times when you know that you want more? You have accomplished much in your career, ministry, or business, but now you are ready for new direction and next level?

Before I took any action, I did what business coaches say to do and that is to identify my "why."

Other reasons "Why" I wanted More

Allow me to give you more insight as to "why" I personally wanted more.

1. I wanted and needed less hours both physically and mentally. I was at the point in my life where I needed to take care of me – physically, spiritually, emotionally, and financially.

2. I wanted to be fully present for my family, especially my son. My son was entering high school and I knew he would need me the most during this time.

3. I wanted more time for ministry. I was able to do ministry during my career; however, it seemed as if I was always being pulled in two directions – my career and my calling. I didn't have support for my ministry work from the leadership. My first boss was supportive because we shared the same values. He was people first and process second. The leadership changed, and my next boss didn't have the same perspective. He was process first and people second. My days were filled, but they started to become less fulfilling.

4. I wanted to own my own business. I wanted to work for myself. I knew it would be hard, but I knew that if others could be a success as an entrepreneur, then so could I!

After coming to the realization that I wanted and was ready for my next level and I was willing to do what it took to get there, I needed my own personal teachable moment. God allowed me that teachable moment by revealing something to me from one of my favorite Bible stories of the Old Testament – the story of Joseph.

Inside-Out from the Story of Joseph

As you will recall from Cheryl's devotional, the story of Joseph is one of family strife, forgiveness, reconciliation, providence, provision, and humility. Joseph was sold to slavery by his brothers who were jealous of his prophetic abilities to analyze dreams and of his being their fathers' favorite. For a while, Joseph found favor in the eyes of the Egyptian slave master and became his trustworthy assistant, but then he was thrown in jail.

Joseph found favor in prison as well. The warden appointed him as his right-hand man. In time, Joseph successfully interpreted the dreams of the king's royal cupbearer and baker who were also imprisoned. Now Joseph was back in the palace successfully interpreting the dreams of the king. Now he was appointed second only to the king himself and was tasked with preparing the nation for years of famine.

The effects of the famine were felt by Joseph's brothers. (Yes! The ones who sold him into slavery.) The brothers heard that there was grain in Egypt. Joseph's brothers traveled there to buy food, not realizing that the man they needed to see was their very own brother.

After two encounters with their brother Joseph (who has assumed an Egyptian name and remained incognito), Joseph reveals his identity to his brothers, restores his relationship with them, and relocates his entire family, including his brothers, to Egypt. After identifying himself as their brother, Joseph tells his brothers,

> *"And now, do not be distressed and do not be angry with yourselves for selling me here, because it was to save lives that God sent me ahead of you"* (Genesis 45:5).

Joseph acknowledges that God positioned him to save the lives of others.

The Teachable Moment of Prayer

Joseph's story of forgiveness revealed to me that next level takes place on the inside (your heart) before it can be manifested on the outside. I realized that a prayer for "next level" actually had four parts.

1. Praying through the pain
2. Praying for heart position
3. Praying for your purpose
4. Praying in your platform

God gave me a diagram to understand it even more.

Beyond Inspiration

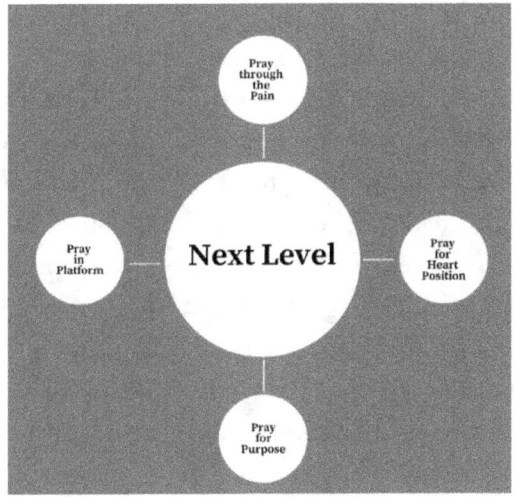

The roadmap to next level is different for everyone. But, the prayer for next level should always focus on the inside (the heart), so that we can see the manifestation of next level on the outside.

How to Pray for Your Next Level from the Inside-Out

Let's review each of the prayers for your next level.

Pray Through the Pain

Whether we want to admit it or not, getting to your next level is going to require some pain. The pain may be in the form of a struggle or a challenge. It may be physical, emotional, spiritual, or even financial pain, but it hurts, nonetheless. Some days, moving to your next level is just hard. Things seem uncertain and your stress gets high. I recall having a terrible situation at work with one of the community college presidents. He called me and told me I was unfit to be a vice-president. I let him talk (mostly he was venting). When I hung up the phone, I began to pray Isaiah 41:10 which says,

> *"Do not fear, for I am with you; do not be dismayed, for I am your God. I will strengthen you; I will help you, yes, I will uphold you with My righteous right hand."*

Every day, I encountered some situation, whether it was small or large, that sent me to my knees. After some reflection, I realized that each situation was a stepping-stone to my next level. What I learned during the pain was preparation for my next. Even though there were days that were difficult to face, I had to learn to pray through all the pain, struggles, and challenges I had to face. I realized my faith is most strengthened, not in the easy times of life, but in the most trying. If you were like me, I know you want getting to the next level to be easy, but sometimes God takes our hand and leads us straight into the darkest of times. However, like Joseph the dark pits of your life are never meant to harm you; but to bring you greater strength, character, trust, beauty, and perseverance. Praying through your pain to get to your next level helps you to become more like Christ. Keep praying through the pain – even if you can't see the next level. God will not leave you in a pit, the same way he did not leave Joseph, but He will walk with you through the pain until you come out on the other side . . .

> Changed.
> Stronger.
> Renewed.
> With great purpose.

Pray for Heart Position

Praying for your heart position is all about praying for your character. You must be in position on the inside so that you can do the work that God has for you on the outside. We do what it takes to be positioned on the outside. We go to classes, get coaching and mentoring, get degrees or certifications. All of these are important, yet we must work on our heart being in right position with God – being ready on the inside. If you're not ready on the inside, then regardless of what you step into on the outside, you're not going to be able to achieve next level. Heart positioning takes shaping and molding your character through trials and tribulations. God has a plan for your life, and He has to develop your character to match His assignment. Your character must match the call God has on your life. Everything you experience really does have a purpose – to get your heart in the right position for your next level. Like Joseph, our heart has to be in right position with God in order for our next level to become a reality.

God will test your character. I recall a woman I considered my sister in Christ saying something to me after church that I took issue with. It hurt me so bad that I started crying. My old nature began to rise. My first desire was to take off one of the red three-inch heel shoes I was wearing and beat her with it. That's how angry I was. I didn't get upset because she had lied on me. What truly hurt me was that she was using this situation to attack my character. I was under attack and I wanted to fight. It was all about my character. I knew the accusations weren't true, and I knew that God would expose the truth eventually, but when the young lady said what she said to me, I didn't stop to think, *What would Jesus do?* My first reaction was, *What is Saundra going to do?* I was headed in the wrong direction. I was about to react in a way that would not have pleased God. My heart would not have been in position with God.

Suddenly out the corner of my eye, I saw a young woman standing on the side of a car. This young woman was assigned to me and I had been ministering to her for some time. She and I had spent hours together discussing how God was maturing her and how she desired to move forward with the call of God on her life. As I continued with my tirade, I could see the look on this young lady's face. It was a look of confusion and disappointment. Then I heard in my spirit, "You're getting ready to crucify your testimony." Immediately my spirit came into alignment with God. My original plan was to fuss one woman out, but God stopped me and showed me where my true focus was supposed to be. My true focus had to be on what He called me to do – regardless of my current situation. When God has a next level assignment for you, He has to develop great character to match that next level. God takes all the time He needs to make you the kind of person He can trust with that next level. Don't assume that the moment He tells you, you are ready for the next level.

When God prepares you, He is making you useful for service. Preparation requires diligence and patience. During preparation, God will shape, strip, purge, and pull you so that He can put in you who you really are. God is positioning your heart. When God prepares you, He positions your heart. God positions and prepares you for your next level. Regardless of what the situations are in your life now, remember that God is preparing you for something far bigger than where you are and everything you are going through is for a purpose. Preparation equips us for the work that God has called us to do. When God starts something in us, He will complete it. God will prepare us, equip us, resource us, shape us, anoint us, instruct us, and transform us so that we will produce fruit for His glory and expand His kingdom. That is the work of the Holy Spirit.

If you're experiencing trials and tribulations, know that God is preparing you for your next level. God isn't simply interested in you getting to your next level; He is interested in you finishing the assignments and accomplishing the thing for which He sent you to do for the next level.

Strong Faith!

Strong Finish!

Pray for Your Purpose

That pain was all a part of positioning your heart for what God has for you. God uses the pain, trials, tribulations, good times, and bad times to position your heart. God doesn't waste anything. So, whatever you experienced in years past, God was using that to position you so that you could stand and walk in your purpose. In order to walk in purpose, you must be in position from the inside. Remember, positioning is an outcome of pain. You will have experiences that cause you to wonder and ask God, "Why am I having to, to deal with this? Why is this happening to me in my life?" Know that God is continuing His positioning of you.

He's using that experience to condition you so that you can walk into your platform God has for you. So, from now on, when you think about position and you think about the experiences and things that are going on in your life, remember to look at every single experience in your life as God positioning you.

When you pray for your purpose, remember that your purpose comes from God. Your purpose comes out of your pain and your heart positioning. God is the only planner for your life; therefore, only He can give you the purpose you have been searching for. Jeremiah 29:11 lets us know that,

> *"For I know the plans I have for you," declares the LORD, "plans to prosper you and not to harm you, plans to give you hope and a future."*

When you pray through the pain, you pray for a heart positioned in God, and you pray for God's purpose for your life, you can have the platform that He designed for you. Whether the platform is a being an entrepreneur, a writer, or a speaker, you cannot be established in the platform until you're walking in the purpose that God has for you.

Pray in Your Platform

Simply put, when you are walking in your purpose, you are on the platform designed for you! Let's make sure that you understand God's platform for you. In the business world a platform is your tribe or expanding your audience or extending your reach or multiplying your influence. Having a nice platform of followers helps to sell books or fill courses that you are selling. Business platforms have their place. But God's platform for you is that you give attention to the things that get God's attention. Prayer, fasting, meditating on His word, and having faith are a few actions that get God's attention. When your platform with God is your focus, your activities, thoughts, and actions will reflect it. As your platform with God grows, you will see yourself begin to influence others.

God commands that we witness to others. Hence, He has given everyone a platform! With that platform is opportunity to do an amazing work for God. An opportunity to amplify the greatness of God in a way that your strength alone will never be able to. God's platform only comes from prayer! Pray each and every day that you give attention to God's platform showing His power and glory in your life.

The Outcomes of Praying for Your Next Level

My experience has shown me that praying for your next level has outcomes. Praying through pain, praying for a heart positioned to God, praying for purpose, and praying for God's platform in your life will bring transformational experiences to you. Because these experiences are different for everyone, I will only list the outcomes without explanations. I believe they are all self-explanatory.

1. Praying for next level will take you into unfamiliar territory and stretch and strengthen you.
2. Praying for next level will take you outside of your comfort zone.
3. Praying for next level will move you to complete trust in God.
4. Praying for next level will give you unfamiliar results.
5. Praying for next level will not give safe results, risks will be required.
6. Praying for next level will require you take actions that you have never taken before.

Don't Let D.O.G.s Keep You from Praying

When God first gave me the vision for the Vision Building Women, my online community, He gave it to me as I was in the midst of doing something else that I knew He had given to me to do. I was in the middle of moving forward with the ministry that God had placed in my heart, so why was there now a vision for next level? Little did I know at the time that everything I was doing was me preparing spiritually, professionally, and personally for the next level that God had for me. God had given me the assignment that He had purposed to move me toward my destiny. But for a while, I was standing in the way of it. How was I in my own way? I was allowing **d**oubt, **o**bstacles, and **g**uilt to keep me from moving forward. I call these the D.O.G.s that will keep you from your new level of destiny.

Let's identify these D.O.G.s and deal with them in prayer.

Doubt will have you uncertain about where God is taking you. You begin to wonder if the next level is really God-given or if it's just something "you want to do." Doubt will eventually lead to fear and discouragement. I have learned that to move forward with the next level, you have to break up with doubt and fear. They can rob you of your joy, peace and the abundance that God has for you. They can also lead to discouragement and have you bogged down with burdens that God never intended for you to bear.

An *obstacle*, by definition, is something that hinders your progress. The very job of an obstacle is to stop you from moving forward. God has a plan for your life. Unexpected obstacles show up in your path and try to stop you from living your purpose and carrying out that plan. No matter what obstacles are currently present in your life, they can't stop the plan God has for you. The greater impact of your purpose and next level, the greater obstacles you will face.

Finally, let's look at *guilt*. I am sure we have all struggled with this one. You feel guilty that you desire your next level. You feel guilty that you are not spending as much time with your family. You feel guilty because someone told you that we're not supposed to dream bigger – we are to be satisfied. I experienced guilt when I moved from having an annual ministry conference to teaching, mentoring, and coaching. Guilt nags us and burdens us until we find some way to shut it down. Guilt is a next level as it becomes a hindrance in your mind.

How do you move forward and get the D.O.G.s out of your life?

1. **Pray! Pray! Pray!** If you have been drowning in doubt and fear and there seems to be insurmountable obstacles all around you trying to stop you, stop and pray. If you feel guilty because you are doing what you have been called to do, then *stop and pray*. Pray for the pain, pray for your heart position in God, pray for your purpose, and pray for your platform. When we give those situations and the people associated with them to God, He will move on our behalf. Also, I learned to stop spending my time listening to others and start maximizing my prayer time.

    Prayer changes things.
Prayer changes you!

2. **Stay connected with people who push your forward.** Remember that the people you hang with have an impact on our lives. You must be careful to choose the people you hang out with, as well as the information with which you feed your mind. We should not share our dreams with negative people, nor feed our dreams with negative thoughts. To keep situations outside from getting inside of you, you have to keep negative, doubtful, fearful, bad-news people out of your life. I know there are people around you that love drama, gossip, and feed off people's struggles. Avoid these people. Instead, spend time with people that encourage you, remind you of your gifts and talents, and challenge you to pursue your vision regardless of the obstacles you are facing. Stay connected to people who keep you sharp and in proper alignment with God.

    Iron sharpens iron.

3. **Stay focused.** If you lose focus, you give up your freedom. Then you fight the wrong battle at the wrong time and for the wrong reasons. Know the battle you are in and fight for it. When you are focused you will receive the prize. The enemy will attempt to distract you and derail you from your purpose. The enemy will make you think you have failed, but you cannot fail, because God does not

create failures. God did not create you to go backwards. Everything about God flows forward! Stay focused on His next level for you.

Move forward!

4. **Upgrade Your Mindset** According to Carol S. Dweck, PhD, author of *Mindset*, "Mindset has become the new psychology of success." How you think about you will influence what you do. This is hard to accept, because accepting this means you must break down walls and at times reinvent who you are. Don't allow yourself to be your biggest obstacle to your next level. The upgrade to my next level was not easy. I was resistant to myself! It took me two years to break free! Often, we think that next level is about more education, bigger career moves, or even who you know that can move you to your next level. These things are good and should not be discounted. However, true and lasting next level is all about prayer and connection to God.

Only God can bring you through the pain of your next level.
Only God can position your heart towards His for your next level.
Only God can determine your purpose for your next level.
Only God can give you His platform of your next level.
Let's pray Isaiah 54:2 for your next level.

> *"Enlarge the place of your tent, and let them stretch out the curtains of your dwellings; Do not spare; Lengthen your cords, and strengthen your stakes."*

Prayer

Heavenly Father, we give you all honor, glory, and praise. God, we give you thanks for who you are in our lives. Thank you for seeing fit to bring us to this point in our lives where we are ready for our next level. Father we pray that You equip us to be able to walk into those things that You had for us to do. God please remove all of the fear and doubt that causes us to hesitate. We thank you Father for the pain that we've had to experience so that we can walk in purpose and on your platforms that you have for us with a heart that is positioned for You.

God, you are stretching us. You have taken us to places that we didn't even know existed. You're getting ready to open doors. Prepare us inside and out for everything that you have for us. Position our hearts and our character so that we can walk and do what you've called us to do. This we ask in Jesus name, Amen.

Questions for Reflection
- Are your thoughts and actions in alignment with your next level?
- When God examines your heart, is it positioned with His?
- Now that you know the path to pray for next level, what will be the components of your prayer life?

Bio:

DR. SAUNDRA WALL WILLIAMS is the CEO of WMS Corporation, a professional development and consulting company that supports emerging and established women leaders to reach the next level in their life, business, ministry, or career. Dr. Saundra specializes in coaching and mentoring women to master their mindset, create unstoppable momentum, and step boldly into the vision and calling on their life at the next level.

A featured speaker, she is the founder of **L.E.A.P. System** and the **Vision Building Institute, Dr. Williams, a** respected authority on individual leadership development is a minister, author, speaker, strategist, trainer, and coach who has a passion for teaching. She left her full-time executive position and turned her passion for leadership into a prosperous enterprise.

Dr. Williams is also an Adjunct Research Professor at North Carolina State University where her teaching focus is Technology and Leadership. An award-winning leader including North Carolina's Technology Woman of the Year, Dr. Williams has a Bachelor of Science in Mathematics, Master of Science in Applied Mathematics and Statistics, and Doctor of Education from NC State University, a Master of Divinity from Regent University, and an Honorary Associate degree from Richmond Community College. She is a certified Chief Information Officer with the State of North Carolina. **Learn more about Saundra Williams at www.drsaundraspeaks.com**

The Next Level of Greatness through Service

Charonda Johnson

As former military personnel, service is huge to me and those I served with. In business and leadership, many think winning means always being on top. As a military superpower, winning meant not being defeated in battle. Yet as a combat warrior, at times winning simply meant having the ability to endure and adapt to whatever challenge I confronted. Often as a believer, I get the feeling that to some winning means living on the mountain top and always being on top.

As a worship leader, we often sing songs with lyrics like, "Lord show me your glory." We want the power, authority, and dominance that comes with walking with God. Yet often we forget that great suffering and endurance was necessary to produce the display of power that we read about in Jesus' life. As I've matured and grown deeper in intimate worship with God, I've come to realize that experiencing God's glory and the weightiness of His presence truly means that you are willing to experience and walk through not only the highs of victory, but also the lows of the valleys of life with Him. In Romans Chapter 8, Paul spoke on this subject. In Romans 8:17-18 he said,

"And if we are [His] children, then we are [His] heirs also: heirs of God and fellow heirs with Christ [sharing His inheritance with Him]; only we must share His suffering if we are to share His glory. [But what of that?] For I consider that the sufferings of this present time (this present life) are not worth being compared with the glory that is about to be revealed to us and in us and for us and conferred on us!" (Amplified bible)

Paul was saying if you want to share in God's glory you must be willing to suffer even as God suffered. Well, how did God suffer? God allowed His only son to be crucified and suffered in agony while watching Him brutally die. Jesus, the Son of God, suffered as He endured separation from His Father while being humiliated to die and atone for our sins on the cross. Jesus laid aside His own desires to partner with God's plan for Himself and all of those who would later reap the benefits of His suffering.

Just like Jesus, when we suffer for the cause of Christ it's important to remember that we are not suffering without a cause or purpose, and we are not suffering alone. Ultimately, as heirs of God, and heirs with Jesus, you and I were created to win! We are partnering with God for a purpose just as Jesus did. Romans 8:28 helps bring us back to the purpose of that suffering. It says,

> *"We are assured and know that [God being a partner in their labor] all things work together and are [fitting into a plan] for good to and for those who love God and are called according to [His] design and purpose. (Amplified)"*

This means that all the suffering, the pressing that we endure, the killing of our flesh and ungodly desires are working together and fitting into a plan for our good. Even the things that you may think or feel are working against you when you partner with God will work in your favor and turn out ultimately to work for your good and in your favor. It's crucial to remember this when confronting the pressures of life, because if you don't it will be easy to lose hope and forget why you are enduring the various trials of life.

In Romans 8: 31-32, Paul gave a reminder that even though at times it may look as if things are working against you, it's critical to remember God is on your side! The God of the universe, the one who made the stars, and everything we see, including the air that we breathe. That same God is on your side and He will give you everything that you need! Paul also gave another bold reminder that God gave us the best that He could give, so it's key to remember that He will not withhold anything from us. I don't know about you, but I can't think of anyone I would sacrifice my son's life for. That's a very serious love and desire to give the best that life can offer. When you think of it from this perspective it makes you realize that God wants to give us the best that He has.

> Romans 8:31 - 32
> *"What then shall we say to [all] this? If God is for us, who [can be] against us? [Who can be our foe, if God is on our side?] [Ps. 118:6.] He who did not withhold or spare [even] His own Son but gave Him up for us all, will He not also with Him freely and graciously give us all [other] things?" (Amplified)*

Now maybe you are thinking, but I thought you said that I was created to win, and now you are talking about suffering. What does suffering, pressure, or endurance have to do with winning? As believers, our warfare is not like that of the world and our victory comes through Jesus. Jesus gained victory over persecution, suffering, sickness, death, and every enemy that we will ever confront in life when He endured the cross, died, and resurrected from the grave. Romans 8:35-37 explains this very well. It says, "Who shall ever separate us from Christ's love? Shall suffering and affliction and tribulation? Or calamity and distress? Or persecution or hunger or destitution or peril or sword? Even as it is written, "For thy sake we are put to death all the day long; we are regarded and counted as sheep for the slaughter. [Ps. 44:22.] Yet amid all these things we are more than conquerors and gain a surpassing victory through Him Who loved us. For I am persuaded beyond doubt (am sure) that neither death nor life, nor angels nor principalities, nor things impending and threatening nor things to come, nor powers, Nor height nor depth, nor anything else in all creation will be able to separate us from the love of God which is in Christ Jesus our Lord." (AMPC)

I believe that God wants us to move to a new level of greatness. He wants to bring us to the point that everything we do and say displays His greatness to everyone around us. This next level of greatness in life will not be achieved through self-promotion, marketing, gaining social media followers, or the traditional methods that we are taught in secular business or leadership. The next level of greatness and winning that I am talking about will manifest as you humble yourself and offer the greatest service possible to those in your circle and sphere of influence. I'm convinced there are two key areas that must be addressed if you want to achieve this next level of greatness. First, you must identify and eliminate areas where pride has been dominant in your life and then you must put on a spirit of service and humility. My hope is that by the time you finish reading this chapter you will be easily able to identify the places in your life where pride is present and determine to clothe yourself with service and humility. In Matthew chapter 20, we see that Jesus was preparing to go up to Jerusalem and he took his 12 disciples with him. The Bible says that he took them aside and began to talk to them explaining what was going to happen to him. He was speaking to them as a prophet as what he was explaining had not yet occurred.

Jesus prophesied his own future. The prophecy He gave wasn't what we would consider a good prophecy or one that in today's world we'd even want to hear, or for that matter would consider as valid from a prophet. He wasn't telling them that he was going to be rich, or promoted, or get a big house. In fact, what Jesus prophesied was the exact opposite of what we often hear from prophets in churches today. The prophecy that Jesus gave for Himself was one that a prophet today would probably get scorned, rebuked, and put out of many churches today. To sum it up, Jesus was telling his disciples listen, I'm about to die for you. I'm going to lay down my life, but on the third day I'm going to get the victory. I'm going to conquer it all when I'm resurrected back to life.

Matthew 20:17 – 28 says, "As Jesus was going up to Jerusalem, He took the twelve [disciples] aside, and along the way He said to them, "Listen carefully: we are going up to Jerusalem; and the Son of Man will be handed over to the chief priests and scribes (Sanhedrin, Jewish High Court), and they will [judicially] condemn Him *and* sentence Him to death, and will hand Him over to the Gentiles (Roman authorities) to be mocked and scourged and crucified, and He will be raised [to life] on the third day. Then [Salome] the mother of Zebedee's children [James and John] came up to Jesus with her sons and, kneeling down [in respect], asked a favor of Him. And He said to her, "What do you wish?" She answered Him, "Command that in Your kingdom these two sons of mine may sit [in positions of honor and authority] one on Your right and one on Your left." But Jesus replied, "You do not realize what you are asking. Are you able to drink the cup [of suffering] that I am about to drink?" They answered, "We are able." He said to them, "You will drink My cup [of suffering]; but to sit on My right and on My left, this is not Mine to give, but it is for those for whom it has been prepared by My Father. And when the [other] ten heard this, they were resentful *and* angry with the two brothers. But Jesus called them to Himself and said, "You know that the rulers of the Gentiles have absolute power *and* lord it over them, and their great men exercise authority over them [tyrannizing them]. It is not this way among you, but whoever wishes to become great among you shall be your servant, and whoever wishes to be first among you shall be your [willing and humble] slave; just as the Son of Man did not come to be served, but to serve, and to give His life as a ransom for many [paying the price to set them free from the penalty of sin]."

In the past when I read this passage, I thought of Jesus' message to His disciples in terms of spiritual gifts rather than recognizing the complete message of what He was trying to convey. I find it very interesting that Jesus was literally instructing His disciples & followers about how He was going to serve them, and they too failed to comprehend what he was trying to convey because before another conversation could start, the mother of one of the disciples was there asking Him to give her sons the greatest and most coveted positions in the Kingdom of Heaven.

Beyond Inspiration

The Bible says that Salome came and kneeled herself and asked Jesus for a favor before she began telling Him to command that her two sons be placed next to Him, on His right and left side. When I picture Salome kneeling in my head, I can't help but think about prayer and worship, because often our posture in prayer and worship is in kneeling. This vision makes me think of how in the past I went to God and have seen others go to God. I know I'm not the only one who has come to God with my personal list of what I wanted in prayer: God, I need a better job. God, I need a bigger house. God, I want more income. God, I want to be married and so on. The vision also makes me think about how in worship, we come kneeling and thanking God for all that He can do for us rather than focusing on who God truly is. Just like this woman, we think that we can manipulate God with our prayer or worship to get what we want, and then we get frustrated when we don't see the results that we've desired or feel that we deserve.

When we come to God expecting Him to move mountains, perform a miracle, or some grand gesture to give us whatever we are seeking, we are just like Salome in this story. We come kneeling physically, but in reality, our hearts are full of pride and truly seeking to manipulate the situations in our favor to get what we want. We are outwardly coming saying, "Hey Jesus I love you. Can you give me some of your goodness? Can I have some of your glory? I want miracles and power Jesus!" Yet, just like Salome, we fail to understand that if we want to carry more of the power and glory of Jesus that we must humble ourselves as He did. We must be willing to die. We have to be willing to endure the crushing and crucible of life. We have to be willing to endure and allow situations and circumstances to crush our will and kill our flesh so that our desires can die and God's glory can be revealed in and through us. This is how we get that next level victory that Jesus achieved when He died on the cross.

It is very prideful that Salome did not come asking Jesus where do you want my sons to sit? Where do you want me to sit or just simply Jesus can I participate and be a part of your kingdom? Instead, she came telling him and commanding Jesus how she wanted it to be in His kingdom. It was very prideful for her to insist that Jesus let each one of her son's sit on His right and left side instead of simply asking where Jesus wanted them to be. Her pride was bold, blatant, and obvious. I believe pride is present whenever, we like Salome, throw our own will and desires to the forefront of our situations instead of God's. Anytime our desires become the priority, pride is at work. Pride was also at work in the disciples in this story, because the Bible tells us that the disciples became resentful and angry with the two brothers. Why would the disciples become angry? They were angry and resentful because they wanted what she was asking for her sons. Now if Jesus' disciples who watched Him heal the sick and raise the dead battled and struggled with pride, how much more do we need to examine our own hearts to ensure that we are living with the true heart of a servant.

I believe pride is in direct opposition of who God created us to be as people who were created in his own image and likeness (Genesis 1:27). Pride often presents itself as more powerful and authoritative than it really is. Pride is rooted in a lie that we are superior to God. When we understand that we carry the image and likeness of God and literally his breath, it is very easy to remain humble because we recognize that all we have literally comes from God (Genesis 2:7). This understanding should make it very easy for us to lay aside our own desires and selfish ambitions for God's.

In this moment in time, Jesus was focused on his purpose which was: SERVICE! He was preparing to make the ultimate selfless sacrifice and literally serve himself up on a platter to be tormented, tortured, brutalized, and martyred for the world! Meanwhile, this good intentioned, well-meaning mother was focused on her goal which was to get herself and her sons a coveted position of authority in the Kingdom of Heaven. Unfortunately, she failed to understand a key Kingdom principle that determines Kingdom Authority. True authority in the Kingdom does

Beyond Inspiration

not come from dominance, prominence, or power. True Kingdom greatness is gained through service and humility. In the kingdom, up does not equal up; up equals down. In fact, the way to elevation and promotion is through humility, and whenever you humble yourself it produces promotion and elevation.

Next, I want to talk to you about what it means to be a servant. This is something that as a combat veteran of the United States Air Force, I have a unique perspective and quite a bit of experience with. In the Air Force we had three core values: Integrity, Service Before Self, and Excellence in All We Do. This literally was ingrained in every fabric of our culture. I want to give you some examples of what service meant for me from a military standpoint. It meant that early in my career when I was in technical training and learning my job that I had to beg for permission to take leave to go for just three days of vacation when my father was having a serious neck surgery. Military trainees were not permitted to take breaks from training because their primary mission was learning how to do their jobs with excellence. Service meant that after 9/11 when my grandmother, who was in her 60s, had a heart attack and had to have seven bypass surgeries that I could not leave my base in New Mexico to travel to Delaware to be with her, because I was on call and needed to be ready to deploy at a moment's notice. Service meant that the military mission had to come first. Service also meant that even though I was already engaged and planning to be married, when my unit was called up to go fight at the start of the Iraq war that my wedding was off the table, and thankfully, it led to the end of that relationship for me. Service meant that when Uncle Sam decided it was time for me to move overseas, even though it was a bit inconvenient for me and I had to leave my family and sell most of my belongings, I did it because I was no longer living my life based on my own desires. I could not do what was convenient for me, because I was under contractual obligation to obey the orders of my Commander in Chief. Service meant that even when my grandmother, a decorated Vietnam War Veteran, died and was going to be buried in Arlington Cemetery, I could not attend her funeral because I had orders to deploy to Iraq.

Just like service in the military, living a life of service to the Lord means that your desires must die and they always take the back seat. I tell my son often that sometimes obedience does not feel good when you are obeying because you want to do the opposite and your flesh is dying, but in the long run it is better to obey because the consequences of disobedience are always costly and even sometimes fatal. Jesus told His disciples if you want to be great in my Kingdom you have to be willing to humble yourself as a servant even to the point of death. Jesus went a step further and literally laid down his life as the perfect example to us all of this servant leader. If you want to step into the next level of greatness, it is essential that you examine and take inventory of yourself with each new task that you choose to take on and answer these simple questions:

- Why are you doing the things you do?
- What is your true motivation to do the things you are doing?
- Who are you serving when you do whatever it is you do?
    - Are you serving God, self, or others?
    - In business, am I more concerned about what my clients or my boss thinks of me or what God thinks of me?
- Who is out serving you in the various areas of your business, ministry, family, marriage, relationships, and life in general?

When you answer these questions honestly you will be able to quickly and easily identify if you are operating in pride or with the heart of a servant. I believe that service is a universal commodity in heaven and earth. I cannot think of any transaction in life or business that does not occur through service. The greatest exchange that ever occurred was when God sacrificed His son for our sins and it occurred through service! Jesus is the greatest example of service to all of us. Let me phrase what Jesus said another way, those that are the greatest in service will be the greatest in life. If you want to be on top: SERVE and out-serve everyone else!

When you make it your mission to focus on being a true servant and offering the best service to those around you, your service will propel you to the next level in business, ministry, relationship, and virtually every area of your life. True ministry is not having a title, being on a platform, or having millions of followers. All of those things are nice to have, but if you are not serving or are providing a substandard service that provides more benefit to you than those you are meant to serve how far will you go, and who will you impact?

If you want to be great you must learn to lay aside pride, and humble yourself by living a life of service. Service is selfless. Service requires self-sacrifice. Service always requires you to be inconvenienced. Service requires commitment and investment. Service will always cost you something, and more times than not it will cost you everything. Living a life of service requires discipline, determination, and perseverance.

I want to challenge you to make the decision right now to live a life of service because living a life of service is the key to greatness. I believe that if you humble yourself and seek the Lord for the areas of your life concerning service, that service will unlock the door for acceleration to your next level in life. Many of the prophets and leaders today are saying this is a time of acceleration for the body of Christ. I personally believe that it's a time of acceleration and advancement, but I believe that this acceleration will only come as we humble ourselves just as Jesus did and lay down our own desires. If we are to experience this next level of advancement and acceleration with Him, we must lay down our own will, desires, and passion, and choose to serve Him completely. I hope that you will let service open doors for you as you move forward into this next level of greatness in your life!

Charonda Johnson

Prayer

Father, I pray for the person that is reading this book. I thank you for allowing them to hear your desire for them to serve as you have served them. We bless you and honor you for your sacrifice for us. Father, your word has said that we should present ourselves to you as living sacrifices in Romans 12. So, we come humbling our hearts and our lives before you. God, in biblical times we know that sacrifices were killed on altars and every sacrifice had to die. We ask you to show us the places in our lives that need to be sacrificed on your altar.

We ask you to search our hearts and show us every part that we have closed off or hidden from you. Please open our eyes and reveal to us the places in our business, marriage, parenting, relationships, and ministry that we have not allowed you to reign. Expose, uncover, and uproot every space where we have not fully surrendered to you, especially the places where pride is present. Show us the places where we have not fully obeyed you. We ask you to speak to us in a way that we will clearly understand. Speak to us now. Speak to us in dreams. God let your message be obvious to us so that we cannot miss what you are revealing in us. Father, I command our ears and our eyes to open to whatever you will expose as we pray.

Father, I pray that you bring back any situations from our past where we've been prideful. We ask you to bring back people and situations to our memory so that we can go back and humble ourselves before you. We thank you that you are King of us all. You are the Lord and ruler, and we give you permission to govern our lives. Show us any place that we are in rebellion to you. I thank you God that you are at work and present in our lives, because you are our creator and God. All that we are comes from you, even our life and breath, and you deserve all that we can give! We come to You humbling ourselves and repenting, asking you to forgive us for being prideful and insisting like Salome to have our own way instead of asking for what you desire for the various situations in our life.

God, we lay aside every weight, sin, any and everything that entangles us and separates us from You. Right now, we choose to run this race that you set before us with patience, persistence, and endurance. We commit to humble ourselves and our desires for Your desires for us. We want what you want for us, and in the places that still have our own desires instead of yours we ask you to create in us clean hearts and renew a right spirit within us. Change us, convict us, and increase our capacity for you and what you want for us. We make the decision that no matter what we face we are willing to suffer, endure, and live a life of service for and with You, so that we can walk and carry your glory and experience the next level of greatness that you are taking us to.

Father, we know that carrying Your glory is not about us. It's not about us rising to the top or shining. The next level of greatness is not for us to sit in the best seat at your right or left hand. The next level of greatness that You are calling us to is all about humility, submission, and even death of our own desires. This is about the sacrifice that you made for us.

We ask you to help us to always remember Your sacrifice for us. Please forgive us for the times that we failed to remember Your sacrifice, your skin that was torn, and the blood that you shed. Jesus you paid a hefty price so that we would live in Your love instead of experiencing Your judgement. When we have moments that pride attempts to dominate our hearts and minds, please help us to remember that everything we have comes from you including our very breath.

Father, I pray that in this season Your Holy Spirit would lead us and guide us in all truth. Holy Spirit, we ask you, take control, and we give you permission to teach us how to serve. God even as you expose and uproot areas of pride in our lives, we ask you to cause us to overflow with Your Holy Spirit.

Father, we don't want to just say words in prayer or sing random songs in worship. We want to pray and sing your heart. We don't want our businesses to just have random products for sale because we want our

Charonda Johnson

products and our services to reflect your heart. So, we ask you to pour your spirit into every place in our hearts, and show us how to serve you with every product and every word from this day forward. I thank you God for this next level that you're taking us to. This place of humility and service to you.

Bio

Charonda resides in Townsend, Delaware with her son and husband, where she is a worship leader and motivational speaker. She began leading worship at the age of 13 with her parents, who most of her life led worship and facilitated music ministry. To Charonda, worship is like breathing, and her greatest passion is to encounter God and lead others into his presence.

Charonda's career includes combat service in the United States Air Force, work for two United States Senators, and work as a Project Manager. She has earned multiple leadership awards in the Air Force and Corporate America. While stationed in Japan, Charonda recorded an album of hymns, and recently she returned to Japan to lead worship and speak. **Learn more about Charonda Johnson by visiting www.facebook.com/MotivateWarrior.**

Acknowledgements

To each of the amazing authors of Beyond Inspiration,
thank you for your yes, your story, and your prayers
to help leaders and entrepreneurs push pass
their boundaries and barriers to create
global impact and influence.

www.ingramcontent.com/pod-product-compliance
Lightning Source LLC
Chambersburg PA
CBHW052034070526
44584CB00016B/2041